N E V E R A G A I N

#NEVER

RANDOM HOUSE
NEW YORK

A NEW GENERATION
DRAWS THE LINE

DAVID HOGG

(Class of 2018)

LAUREN HOGG

(Class of 2021)

**MARJORY STONEMAN
DOUGLAS HIGH SCHOOL
PARKLAND, FLORIDA**

THIS BOOK IS DEDICATED TO

THE PARKLAND SEVENTEEN.

AND TO VICTIMS OF

GUN VIOLENCE EVERYWHERE.

WE WILL NEVER FORGET.

CONTENTS

#NEVERAGAIN

1.

VALENTINE'S DAY

WHEN YOU OPEN YOUR EYES BUT THE NIGHT-
mare doesn't go away, you've got no choice but to
do something. Our first job now is to remember.
Our second job is to act. Remember, act, repeat.
Since that day, none of us are the same. But we
are alive. And in memory of those who are not,
we will remember and act for the rest of our lives.

We've always been taught that as Americans,
there is no problem that is out of our reach; that
if we set our minds to it, we can solve anything.
Anything except for our problem with gun violence. That can't be fixed. When that problem
flares, it's "Hey, wow, that's terrible. Too bad
there's nothing to be done about it." Like it's an
act of God, or a natural disaster, something be-

yond our control that we are helpless to do anything about. Which defies all logic and reason.

We live in Florida, a place which has some experience with natural disasters. What happened on Valentine's Day 2018 was neither natural nor an act of God. What happened that day was man-made—which means that as human beings, we have the capacity to do something about it.

Our generation has the *obligation* to do something about it.

In class, we learned about something called entropy. I guess you could say that entropy came to our school that day, and since the shootings, we have seen that there are powerful forces that thrive in chaos. Entropy is what the universe wants to happen. The story of existence and human civilization is the struggle against entropy—working to stick together, not fly apart. To cooperate, not fight. To love, not hate.

But I'm getting ahead of myself.

I can't speak for everyone. If I was my freshman or sophomore or halfway-through-junior-year self, I would just sit here and explain everything. That's how pretentious and overconfident I was, and probably still am, to some extent. But if there's one thing I learned from the shootings, it's that my freshman or sophomore or halfway-through-junior-year self couldn't have survived that day. That's the reason for this book—we all had to find a way to survive, and we all had to come up with our own answers, but it turned out that all of our answers were just different facets of the same answer. That's why the shootings made us stronger instead of destroying us.

So I could sit here and tell you the heroic tale of a kid who was so cool under fire and so passionate about justice that he whipped out his camera while the shooter was still shooting. But the truth is that I was thinking about something one of my teachers had been talking about a couple of days before: in the sweep of time billions of people have lived on this planet, yet the world only remembers a few hundred of them. This means that everybody else is just a background character who will be forgotten into the nothingness that is time and the universe. My teacher was talking about being humble, but I'm way too

myopic and self-involved for that. My thinking
went more like this: "Am I going to be just another background character? Is this what it's all
been leading up to? Just a bullet to the head?"
And I decided, "Okay, I may be another background character, but if I'm going to die I'm
going to die telling a damn good story that people need to hear."

That's why I hit record. I was almost acting out
the role that a journalist plays in a war zone,
where you have to ask these questions and stay
focused on one simple thing. That's what kept me
calm. And to be honest, except for one split second when the fear rushed through me, I really
thought it was just a drill. Even after we knew it
wasn't a drill, it was still so hard to accept the reality of it.

But here's the important thing: my sister, Lauren, was fourteen that day, and there's nothing
myopic or self-involved about her. After the
shooting stopped, she was crying so hysterically
that I didn't want to be around her. Her friends
had been murdered, and I couldn't stand being

helpless to ease her pain. You could even say that's how this whole movement started, at least for me—I was trying to avoid my sister.

That's why I knew I couldn't write this book alone. So I'm going to shut up now and let her take it from here.

WELL, I GUESS I'LL START off with the day that it all happened. It was February 14, Valentine's Day. If I had to describe the overall feeling before it started, I'd tell you that it was a great day. Everybody was just so happy, giving each other chocolates and flowers and hugs, it was like the whole school was glowing. I remember joking with my friends like, "Oh my God, if I see another couple asking each other out, I'm gonna barf."

When the fire alarm went off, I was in TV Production, my last class of the day. We'd already had a fire drill that morning, so we thought it was just a Valentine's Day prank. Everybody was laughing, and we took our time packing up our bags. I still remember yelling at my friend Sam to hurry up because we were taking forever, and it's really weird for me to think that just across the campus, total hell was going on.

The first time that I kind of realized something was wrong was when we got to the bottom of the stairwell, because I looked out the window and across the bus loop and saw all this movement and realized that kids were running. Just from the look in those kids' eyes, I knew something was wrong. I can't really describe it any other way than it was like a movie. Everything just seemed so bright. But the teachers had told us we were going to have a drill with blanks being fired and actors running around and kids pretending they'd been shot and stuff, so every kid around me was laughing and joking with their friends. But somehow inside of me, I knew something was really wrong. The other kids' faces . . . it's awful to describe that look in their eyes. And I remember turning and glancing down the hallways and seeing more kids run by with their roses and their chocolates, girls screaming and boys just crying like I've never seen before. Everybody around me thought it was a joke but I knew, I knew something was wrong. So I grabbed my four closest friends from that class, and even though they were smiling and stuff, I remember yelling, "Guys, something's wrong here." And they were like "Lauren, it's just a joke, it's just a drill."

But I was so scared. I remember looking around me and paying really close attention to my surroundings because our dad's an FBI agent and he's been in shootings before, so literally every single time we'd go into a movie theater or mall, our parents would tell us to make sure we know where the exits are and if anything happens, to make sure to breathe. "Try to relax so you don't panic."

I was born in 2003, so Columbine happened before I was born, 9/11 happened before I was born, and I've grown up since kindergarten with code-red drills. My generation has been trained to deal with things like this.

So even though I'm usually really anxious, I went into this weird mode of calm. I was just so determined to get back to our TV Production classroom because I knew we would be safest there. I was trying to run up the stairs as fast as I could, but all these juniors and seniors were like, "Stop running, guys, it's fine." When I was finally almost back to that classroom, I saw the librarians standing in the hallway, and all of a sudden their walkie-talkies were going off and they were listening to something, and then I just saw their faces go pale, and one librarian started screaming, "Code red! Code red! Everybody get back to your classrooms now!"

And kids still thought it was a joke. They were *laughing*. That was how routine these drills had become. Or maybe it was more that the mind doesn't want to believe what it doesn't want to believe. We got back to my class, and my teacher had told us that if anything ever happened, we should go to the farthest room, which in TV Production is a tiny little room where they film the news. We were trying to open the door, but for some reason, the door was locked. So the three of us who thought it was real started freaking out, and we ran to the teacher's desk and started digging around through the drawers trying to find a key. Finally, our teacher, Mr. Garner, came in and he was like, "Guys, this is serious."

We opened the door to the back room, and the kids flooded into this tiny little space. My brain went into this mode where I was just completely determined to get into the safest place possible, so I grabbed my four close friends and said, "Guys, I'm not overreacting, we need to hide." We have this set where there's a little pocket in the corner, so we slid behind this board with nails sticking out into this little corner. By that point, we were all in shock. We just couldn't think about what was going on, we were so scared and trying so hard to be as quiet as we could be. But there were these two kids who still thought it was a joke, and they were laughing. We wanted to yell at them to be quiet, but we thought it would defeat the purpose, because if the shooter was walking down our hall he would hear us.

The worst part about hiding, for me at least, was when we started getting texts. *Oh my God, what's that noise?* one read. *It sounds like somebody's shooting.* And the next one read, *Someone's run-*

ning down our hall with a gun shooting. I love you guys so much! And then another person wrote, *Someone's shooting into my class, there's smoke in the air, it's so thick.* Then came videos of people dying on the floor, people bleeding out, and nobody knew who they were because it was so blurry and their hair was covering their faces.

Then a kid with us managed to pull up the local news on his phone, so we were all watching the helicopter footage of kids running out of our school building. The headline was SHOOTER AT STONEMAN DOUGLAS HIGH SCHOOL, PARKLAND, FLORIDA—POSSIBLE INJURIES. I was sitting on the floor with my friends in that corner behind the board, holding hands, and I remember my friend Sam saying over and over again, "We're gonna be another number. I don't want to be another number." And kids were saying, "Do you think we're even gonna get on the news?" We didn't know how many people were dead at that point. But that look in people's eyes, us having to text our parents, *I love you guys so much, there's a code red, there's a shooter at my school.* There were kids who had never even talked to each other before holding hands, quietly saying, "I love you." I watched my friends crying but trying to stay quiet, trying to keep themselves from screaming or whimpering so the shooter wouldn't be able to find us. Just as I was trying to text my family my phone died, which was horrific.

We were packed into that little room for three hours, just sitting there and holding hands and not knowing what to do. Through our group chat, the news flooded into our hiding place: *Oh my God, he's shooting down our hallway.* And other messages that said, *He's shooting into my room . . . I love you guys so much . . . Tell my parents I love them.* And, *Oh my God, our teacher's dead, bleeding out on the floor.* The absolute worst was, *Oh my God, I think Alyssa's dead.*

Alyssa was my friend.

Finally we heard someone running down our hall. We thought it was the shooter because there were so many rumors going around—there are three shooters, they're in this building, in that building. Kids' faces were just in shock, and the others started trying to squeeze into the corner where we were hiding, and they were sitting on top of us, so many kids that they started knocking over TV equipment and it was falling on us and kids were certain they were about to die, and were trying to suppress their screams.

Then we heard somebody bang on the door really hard, and we all got so scared. Seconds later, they kicked the door open and shouted, "SWAT! SWAT!" They told us to get out from where we were hiding and get our bags, then put our hands up in the air and walk out in a line, single file.

I remember the look on my teacher's face as he was making sure every kid was there. He was like, "It's okay, Lauren, you're safe, it's over." And just him trying to reassure me . . . Things were so horrific and surreal. It's just so hard to think something like that is really happening, even as it's happening to you.

They did a head count as we were walking out of the building—"Are you injured? *Are you injured?*" Then they gave us all numbers. I was number ninety-one. And just knowing that I was ninety-one, that was my number, and they were telling us to get in a straight line with our hands above our heads again and walk out of the school, remembering how we were so happy before it started, it was now just all so weird and unreal. And when we were finally almost out, down the last hallway, all of a sudden they said, "Run! Run! Run!" We still didn't know what was going on, we didn't know if it was another shooter, so we all ran with our backpacks on and our hands above our heads, literally running for our lives and looking to see who was there and if any of our friends were missing. And the absolute worst—actually, I don't want to talk about that yet.

When we got to the parking lot, I saw parents running down the streets from all angles, coming to find out if their kids were all right. And I saw my dad, and it was like the best feeling ever. That was when I finally lost it. Just hugging him and knowing only that morning, saying goodbye to my dad and mom, it could've been the last time I saw them, and seeing all the parents who didn't know whether their kids were alive or not—it wasn't just us running for our lives that day, but it was our parents, too. The helplessness I felt, I can't even imagine what the parents felt. Everything seemed so bright and hot and loud, all ambulances and fire trucks and cop cars and kids being put into ambulances, making these horrific sounds. And my dad was crying so much, just saying, "I love you, Lauren" over and over, "I love you so much.... I'm so glad you're here."

The absolute worst? That was when I got home, when the weight of what had happened began to hit me. I know that sounds weird because I made it home and I was safe, but I wanted to see what was happening and my parents went to David's room because they hadn't talked to him yet. So I got up and changed the channel to the news. All of a sudden I started seeing the faces, just like when other horrific tragedies happen and you see the victims and think, "Oh, that's so sad, those poor people." But when you see the faces of your friends on the TV and hear that they're being pronounced dead or missing—they said they were missing, but I knew they weren't missing, they were dead—that was when something inside me just broke. I was screaming and wailing like a possessed person because for the first time in my life, death became real to me.

And this was not just death, this was murder—
mass murder. My mom said the sound that came
out of my mouth was "subhuman." She even tried
to get me to take a shot of whiskey because she
didn't know what else to do.

That was when David said he was going back
to the school. I know he says it was about how I
was crying, but he's my older brother and he's always tried to protect me. I think he felt helpless
and couldn't deal with it—he has this personality
where his way of dealing with stuff is by getting
things done. And he's a journalist, too, so he knew
how things would probably go. He said, "I have
to go. I need to tell the reporters what happened."
And my parents physically tried to stop him. My
dad closed the door and said, "We are not allow-
ing you to go back to that school." But David was
just so determined. He said, "Dad, I need to do
this. If they don't get any stories, this will just
fade away. I have to make sure this stays in the
news." So finally, my parents kind of gave in and
told him, "Well, we're not going to drive you."
And David said, "Okay, I'm taking my bike."

And that was how everything started.

——

BEFORE WE GO ANY FURTHER, I have to interrupt Lauren and tell you that I think her last sentence gets it wrong. From my point of view, what really happened was that I said a lot of things in front of the cameras that night—it's all a blur now so I can't even remember most of it. But all the media people picked the same sound bite: "We're the kids, you're the grown-ups. Please do something." And when I said that, I was thinking about Lauren. It's almost like I was so numb and angry, I needed her to feel for me.

So you could say everything began with her howling at our TV, but that wouldn't be true, either. Anger will get you started but it won't keep you going, so I'm pretty sure I would have burned out after a few days or weeks. The real beginning came two days later at Cameron Kasky's house. I didn't even know him that well, but he invited an amazing collection of people to his home, and a few others were so moved to act that they just showed up on their own. I want to say their names: Delaney Tarr, Ryan Deitsch, Jaclyn Corin,

Sarah Chadwick, Alex Wind. And Emma González, the beating heart who keeps us all sane.

That's why I said I can't speak for anyone but
myself. Lauren and I are telling our story to show
you how we grew up into people who felt like we
had to do something and could do something.
We definitely think that's valuable information,
and we hope that seeing things through our eyes
will give you ideas of your own. Because none of
us can do this alone and we need you, basically.
But we're all really different people. We don't
even have the same opinions on gun control. The
only thing we share completely is what Lauren
said when she was getting started—we were all
born after Columbine, we all grew up with Sandy
Hook and terrorism and code-red active-shooter
drills.

We all have grown up conditioned to be afraid.
And we're all sick and tired of being afraid.

2

CANDY CANE LANE

WHY US? WHY NOW? AFTER SO MANY SCHOOL shootings when people just shrugged and moved on, or offered their "thoughts and prayers" and moved on, what gave a group of teenagers at Marjory Stoneman Douglas High School the idea that they could actually change things?

We get that question all the time. Cameron came up with the "mass-shooting generation" idea, which is definitely part of it. Another part is that we are growing up in a time when technology gives us the confidence to assume that we can do things and figure out the world in ways that it hasn't been figured out before. No permission necessary. Stoneman Douglas is a big piece, too, because the teachers there put such a huge emphasis on studying real problems in the world today, so we already knew a lot about politics and social issues and just presumed that we could do something about them. And you can't overlook privilege. We are mainly middle-class white kids with higher expectations than probably most people in our age group. But we all have a lot of really personal reasons, too, and those might be the most important reasons of all.

For Lauren and me, growing up in California was a big part of it. We lived in a little beach town about ten miles south of LAX, the Los Angeles International Airport, an ordinary place in every way but one—our neighborhood. All the streets around where we lived were named after the developer's children, and every Christmas, our subdivision was transformed into "Candy Cane Lane." Our neighbors went nuts. Their Christmas displays didn't stop at the ends of their lawns, they kept going across the street and lights climbed high up into the trees. Parents from all over Los Angeles would bring their kids to see it, thousands of them walking right by our windows every night. If you got up high enough to look down on it from above—I've always liked being up high and seeing the hidden patterns—our neighborhood must have looked like one giant Christmas display. Or a nervous system with some kind of infected node.

Lauren remembers it as magical. Whenever the subject comes up, the first thing she mentions is our dad's homemade Christmas lawn ornaments. You see, the house came with about a dozen ceiling fans that my parents had taken down when we'd moved in, but our dad being our dad (and a former Navy helicopter pilot), he just couldn't throw them out. He's really frugal. I mean really, really frugal. So he built these helicopters and put stuffed animals in them and hung them from the tree outside. The fans still worked, so the propellers would turn. Kids loved them— "Look, Mommy, it's a helicopter!"

I concede the magic. But inside, we were freezing our asses off. Our house had inadequate central heating, mostly just a space heater in my parents' bedroom, so pretty much every night of the winter I'd have to sleep on the couch in front of their bed with Lauren's feet in my face. Every

morning I would get up, run to the shower, turn
it on, get back on the couch and grab the space
heater and huddle around it like it was some kind
of radioactive egg I was trying to hatch, then run
to the shower again and spend fifteen minutes
under the now warm water, defrosting to the
point where I could feel my fingers—I wish I was
kidding—then get out and run back to the space
heater. I still remember the smell of iron coming
off the coils and the promise I made to myself:
"When I'm older, I'm going to live in a house
with heat."

People ask why our folks didn't just get better
central heating, which strikes me as a perfectly
reasonable question. The answer is that it would
have cost something like ten thousand bucks and
our dad just couldn't bring himself to part with
the cash. The official excuse was that they were
both public servants—Mom's an elementary-
school teacher—but I move to submit those ceiling fans into evidence. Yes, Dad is a super nice
person and liked to stand in the window and
watch the kids enjoying themselves, but when
you run a cost-benefit analysis on the time it took

to build decorations versus the cost of store-bought decorations, the only logical conclusion is that he just couldn't stand to throw them out.

On the plus side, Lauren and I realized early that we had to find a way to make our own money. We had to adopt an entrepreneurial approach to the world. I think it was my idea to sell cookies to the Christmas-lights crowd, but Lauren was the sales genius. We got our mom to buy the cookies at the supermarket, dumped them out of the bag, wrapped them individually, and sold them from a table in the front yard. With all those thousands of people walking by, business was good. Then Lauren realized she could exploit her looks, because she had these blond ringlets and dimples, and people would stop to admire her like she was some kind of human Christmas ornament herself. So she started selling things way over price. We went from one dollar a cookie to two dollars and then three dollars, then we started selling five-dollar bottles of water we bought at the store for a buck. The traffic was really bad getting out, so people would get thirsty or hungry and buy something from the adorable children under the helicopter tree. Then one day we ran out of water and cookies, and Lauren went into the house, told our mom she was hungry, and came back out with one of those little snack bags of chips moms put in their kids' lunch bags. She sold it for ten dollars. She ran back inside and did some adorable begging and came out with another one and sold that one, too. We started making hundreds of dollars every night, which definitely cemented us as a team, "partners in crime" is the way she likes to put it. Our parents had no clue—until Lauren blew our cover because she was obsessed with buying a stupid doll.

Wait, I stand corrected. The doll was Jessie from *Toy Story 2,* she says, and it was a very cool doll. The problem was, it cost fifty dollars. Mom said she was sorry but there was no way. "You'll simply have to wait until your birthday, Lauren." So Lauren just whipped out her wallet and peeled off fifty bucks. She says Mom's jaw "literally dropped to the floor." She looked at my sister as if to say, *Who is this kid of mine?*

All that stuff is normal family life, though. We didn't realize that our family was so different until years later. Doesn't every dad wear a gun on his belt every day?

Sometimes I would go into the garage with him when he cleaned it, and I'd sit there watching him. Seeing how careful and serious he was, I always knew a gun was a tool. It was never a toy. You had to be very responsible with it. It could kill people. But we also knew it was something he needed to do his job and stay safe.

The shooting incident at LAX—where a gunman shot several people and killed a TSA agent—drove that home, because our dad's office was in the terminal where it happened and we knew the police officer who shot the gunman. He was one of our family friends.

Dad would usually leave home at six in the morning and come back at six at night, go upstairs, shower, come back downstairs in his white T-shirt and torn pants, eat dinner in front of the TV with all of us, and then go back out to work some more, sometimes multiple times in one night. So we knew the news was important. We'd eat in front of the TV and watch *ABC World News Tonight with Diane Sawyer* every single night. And it so happened that one night, the news was about a shooting incident that involved our dad. That was why we both believed in the Second Amendment. We were glad he had that gun. And we still believe in it. And Dad still has guns. We have guns in our house right now.

But what I've learned since LAX is that it can be very hard to change what people believe about the Second Amendment. Some people just love to think we have a secret plan to sneak up and take away their guns. No matter how many times we say it isn't true, they just won't believe us. I think they actually kind of enjoy being paranoid, to tell you the truth.

Anyway, having guns in the house and treating them responsibly was just a fact of our lives when we were kids, and I didn't really think about it much. I was too busy being a pain.

The word "difficult" came up a lot to describe me. "Slow learner," I was called at school. I didn't learn to read until fourth grade. Eventually we figured out I had dyslexia, but I never bought that as an excuse for everything because I was difficult from day one.

When I was in kindergarten and nobody knew how to read, Mom and Dad bought me a Spider-Man bike, but I wouldn't let anyone teach me how to ride it. Just because my mom suggested it, I refused to do it. By third grade, I still hadn't even tried once.

I would just turn everything into an us-versus-them situation. Some of it, I think, was because Dad worked so hard that we were basically growing up in a matriarchy. And our mom is stubborn as steel. She does not move. So maybe I was emulating her.

I'm not saying the dyslexia had nothing to do with it. Getting pulled out of class every day to go to special ed classes was annoying and embarrassing, and I remember one of my first-grade teachers telling my parents that I would amount to nothing, like I was some kind of broken toy. But I knew I'd be good at something, business probably, so those teachers who had no faith in me really just made me stronger. They taught me not to give a shit about what other people think—all that matters is what you think.

The worst part about the dyslexia thing was

feeling like I was a big disappointment to my parents. My reaction? Instead of making any kind of effort to do better, I worked hard to be a disappointment. For example, our mom would try to take me to sailing lessons or golf lessons, all these things that were supposed to be fun, and I would fight her every time. "Golf lessons? Um, no. Why would I want to do that?"

I didn't want to be turned into anything; I just wanted to be a kid and have fun. I wanted to go to the beach and ride my boogie board. Dyslexia hadn't been my idea—why were all these people treating me like I was defective? So I became more and more narcissistic and basically turned into a jerk. Like one morning in second grade, I distinctly remember getting up and looking at this striped shirt in my closet and thinking, "I'm just gonna be a little shit today. Let's see who I can piss off."

I guess you might say that I am a born contrarian. The good part of that is stepping back from normal-kid life allowed me to find my own way to do things that I could be good at. For example, at the baseball field there was this hidden bench that somebody had stuck in a tree years ago and the tree grew around it. I would sit up there during baseball season and watch the other kids play every day—from a good eight feet above the field, where nobody could see me.

At some point, I saw a way to make some money. During the baseball season you could turn in foul balls to get twenty-five cents or a hot dog or whatever, and from that bench in the tree I could see how balls kept getting trapped in this huge patch of ivy behind the home-run fencing. The kids would go looking where the balls went in but didn't realize they could roll down the hill under the ivy. I would wait until everybody left and walk up and down the ivy, searching in a grid pattern, using my feet as sonar essentially, to find these nasty-ass baseballs that had been there for years, then take them home on my bike, wash them off as well as I could, and go back the next day, right up to the most naïve parent volunteer I could find and say, "Here's six baseballs, I'll take the nachos, please."

Third grade was when things started to turn around a little. I had a teacher who had a lot of faith in me, Ms. Jackson, and I was starting to sort of have a little faith in me, too. So one day I just woke up and thought, "I'm going to do it. I'm going to ride my bike." I asked my dad—it was Father's Day—if he would teach me, and he took me to the parking lot at the local elementary school. Within five minutes, I was riding without training wheels. The next day, we rode from my house to LAX and back, over thirty miles. My dad couldn't walk for the next two weeks.

Now I had a good "outlet for my energy," as they say. I rode my bike so much I have two different sized thumbs. Seriously. Because when I outgrew the Spider-Man bike, my dad got me a new bike from Costco that I basically snapped in half—I wanted to be a cool mountain-biking kid and get my bike all dirty, so I built a little dirt-biking circuit with a few jumps and dips and went around it thousands of times, again and again. And my dad being super cheap, he refused to buy me a new bike. I didn't have that kind of money so my only option was my mom's really trashy thirty-year-old bike from college, which had a broken gear. So I had to hold the gearshift all the time, and after a couple of years, my thumb stopped growing. Jump forward about six years and one day I look down and go, "Wait a second, why are my thumbs different?"

The funny thing is, there came a point when I could have bought a new bike, but I just never thought about it. The bike I had worked, more or less. But when the GoPro came out, I had to have one of those. A camera you can stick on your helmet? How cool is that? But how could I raise the money?

Well, December was coming up. Which meant Christmas lights and helicopters and thousands of people walking past our house. So I went out and bought some glow sticks and glow paint and candy, and I wrote GLOW STICKS AND CANDY FOR SALE AHEAD on the sidewalk in glow paint. I marked everything up two hundred percent so I'd get two dollars for a glow stick that cost a dollar, made around five hundred dollars, and bought the GoPro with half of it. The rest I invested in a stock portfolio with my mom and a friend. We had Tesla, Southwest, and two 3D printing companies. We just sold it this year and more or less doubled our money.

That sign about glow sticks and candy ahead is still there, by the way. It just will not go away. I went back last summer and told the new kids, "You know who wrote that? This guy." Thank God, it's all spelled correctly!

The next thing was drones. When those started coming out, the thought of taking the camera on my head and sending it into the air was the most exciting idea ever. It was my bench in the baseball tree times a thousand. And once I got it, it didn't take long for me to try to find a way to monetize it. Pretty soon I was getting a hundred bucks a set for pictures of houses from above, and I was just fourteen. I would tell other kids, "I have my own drone company, I don't need a job like you guys."

Thinking of that now, I cringe. But that's not the most insensitive thing I did. There was this girl in middle school who liked me, and I just led her on, letting her think we were boyfriend and girlfriend, and then I started going out with someone else and never said anything. I was just such an immature walking hormone. I'm still embarrassed every time I think of it.

I was just so narcissistic and pretentious back then, even more than I am now. The only good thing I can say is that pretentiousness was probably my substitute for actual confidence. And that turned into me wanting to take debate. I always liked talking, so it seemed cool to win something just by talking. But realistically, I was a special ed kid who was taking remedial English and there was something like thirty people trying out for ten positions on the debate team, so I probably wouldn't have done it if I hadn't been so full of myself.

Somehow, miraculously, I made the team. Up until then, I'd never done much homework. "Fake it till you make it" was my thinking. But with debate I started getting up early and riding my bike to school, two miles every morning, and I realized how good it felt to put that kind of effort into something educational. And I found out I was good at debate. Those kids who got As and took advanced classes? In debate, I could kick their asses.

Put all that together and everything was going spectacularly. By eighth grade, I was the happiest I'd been in my life. I even thought I'd found a girl I loved. And that was when my parents said we were going to move to Florida. I was so pissed off, I cannot even begin to tell you.

But I've been going on so much about my childhood problems that I skipped right over Sandy Hook. It was late 2012, just before Christmas of my seventh-grade year, and we were watching the news, as usual, when the first reports came out. My parents were so stunned, saying, "This is crazy," again and again, that I realized that it wasn't normal. Which meant that all the code-red drills we'd been having weren't normal, either. I thought, "How could something like this happen?" I remember posting about it on Instagram: *This is a sick guy.*

Then I forgot about it. Like everybody else.

Same thing with the shooting at LAX a year later. Even after I heard it happened in the terminal where Dad's office was, I still bought into the idea that this wouldn't affect me. And my dad was involved in the crime-scene investigation! I knew some of the FBI agents who were directly involved—my dad's co-workers. Even still, it hadn't happened directly to me, and so ultimately it was forgettable. I don't know if that's a human thing or just an American thing, but avoidance and forgetting were central to the America of my upbringing.

Until, of course, that all changed.

That's pretty much all I have on California. Now Lauren's going to tell you how I got everything wrong.

FIRST OFF, DAVID WASN'T that mean. I think he overdramatizes that. I'm not sure why, because he was always nice. He's a great older brother. I remember one time when these big scary fifth-graders took my soccer ball and I was crying, David said, "Tell me who it is, I'll go get it from them, and I'll make sure they won't do it to you again." And they didn't.

I was protective of him, too—we were like a tag team for getting through life. When people made fun of him because he couldn't read, calling him stupid and stuff, I'd tell them to stop making fun of my brother. I was so offended and angry. David is one of the smartest people I know. Before he learned to read, even in second grade, he would listen and take notes on whatever the teacher said. He would sit there for hours and listen to the news so he knew as much about politics as most adults. My mom jokes that David was born at forty.

I do remember the shooting at LAX, which made a big impression on me because of my mom pulling me out of class. I was like, "Why is Mom here? She's supposed to be teaching her own class right now." And I very vividly remember her telling me, "Lauren, your dad's in a shooting at the terminal. I think he's okay but I didn't get a text from him." Like David said, they hid nothing from us. And she told me, "Lauren, don't tell anybody else because their parents might work at the airport and they might get scared." And I was so scared! But looking back, I think she put me in the position of an adult. Even though the other kids were the exact same age as me, I had to protect them.

When my dad got home that day, even though

I was so young, I remember thinking, "Oh my God, that could've been the last time I saw my dad."

Sandy Hook happened around the same time, when I was seven or eight, so it all must have gotten connected in our minds with Dad's lessons— "Lauren, if you ever get into a bad situation, just stay calm, don't freak out, be determined, find where to hide, and you will survive." Our mom did it, too. Every single time we went to a movie theater or a mall, she'd say, "Make sure you locate the exits."

But life back then wasn't so deadly serious, and we didn't yet feel so responsible for the problems of the world. And as David says, we had a child's capacity to forget. Every single day in the summer, we would wake up, go to the beach, get snacks from the snack shop, and hang out with our friends, just lying in the sand all day and watching the surfers. Then we'd run into the freezing water and then charge up the beach to where the sand was warm. We would just spread out on the warm sand, and it felt so good. David would be boogie boarding for hours and hours, and whenever we got hungry or thirsty we'd walk to this little shopping center that had Trader Joe's, Jamba Juice, and Yogurtland—we got Yogurtland every day. Then we we'd go home and take a nap and it was the best nap ever because we were so tired. That was the life.

David would always talk about having all the windows open with a cool breeze coming through, how it would get misty and foggy at night and Mom would be making something that smelled really good. Living at the beach gave us the idea that life could be awesome and it should be awesome. The worries of the world could wait.

To me, even though he didn't talk about it, that was a big part of why David got so upset when they told us we were leaving for Florida. I was kind of excited at first because I'd never moved before and they showed us these brochures of Disney World. But David was literally screaming up the stairs, "I don't want to move to Florida! I'm not moving!"

I think it was just the age difference. Because he was in high school already—we left in December, in the middle of the school year, just when the lights came out on Candy Cane Lane—and he had some really good friends and a girlfriend.

But our parents had made up their minds, especially Mom. Because Dad had incipient Parkinson's disease and Florida was cheaper, plus the FBI would pay for the move and let him retire there. When David realized there was no way out of it, he got really angry. He was like, "Fine! But I'm getting a computer, I'm choosing my room, I'm picking the color!" He had so many demands for moving, but Mom just went along with them.

And that was really important, too—David always knew that if he had a decent reason and pushed hard enough, he could be very persuasive.

When our last day came, I remember going into my room and just not recognizing it. It looked so empty. It kind of hit me all at once— "it's real, we're really leaving." Then we closed the door for the last time and drove down the street, and I was crying so much that the Christmas lights looked all blurry.

3.

PARKLAND

MOVING IN THE MIDDLE OF A SCHOOL YEAR sucks.

Lauren just reminded me that when we got to Florida, I shouted at my parents, "I don't want to live here! I don't want to live here!" I think it was the weather that put me over the top—just walking out of the airport, it hit me like a hot burp from Satan that was moist and smelled like the Everglades, which is not a good thing to smell like. We weren't close to the beach, either, so goodbye to boogie boarding. So my mom said, "Fine, live under the stairs"—because there was a little door under the stairs just like the one in Harry Potter—and I said, "Fine, I'm going to live under the stairs!" What a jerk, right?

School didn't help because (*a*) I had no friends, and (*b*) Marjory Stoneman Douglas is a really competitive school. Turned out all those years of blowing off my homework wasn't such a great idea. Who knew?

Lauren says a lot of it was just being a freshman. "It's the time when we have the key but can't get in the door yet." Which is classic Lauren because she nails it and forgives it at the same time.

So there I was, trying to open the door. It happened that I had two great classes, TV Production and Debate, topics I was really interested in, so combine that with a lonely kid who had a lot of time on his hands in an unfamiliar place and a really competitive school—at Stoneman Douglas, in our generation, it's almost like a badge of honor to be stressed out about grades and getting into college. If you want to be really cool, you have to be depressed and cynical and witty. We're Generation Stress. So when you have basically spent your whole life on a boogie board, that's like getting shocked out of a coma. "We're losing him! Clear! Clear!"

This is going to sound funny, but John Oliver

kind of saved me. He's just so hilarious and he goes really deep, which taught me that beneath any news story there are many layers of complexity. The first episode I saw was about all the sugar in processed food. For some reason, he wanted the food companies to rate sugar content in terms of peanuts, so it ended with, "If you're going to shove your peanuts into our mouths, the very least you could do is tell us what we're swallowing!" Perfect freshman humor, right? I laughed my ass off, which probably made my parents happy. "Don't know what he's doing in there, but at least he's not threatening to live under the stairs." John Oliver did another one that year on Citizens United, the Supreme Court's "money is speech" decision, where they basically told rich people it was legal to buy politicians. It doesn't take a rocket scientist to extend that to the NRA getting more and more radical—and more and more powerful.

Hank Green's *SciShow* on YouTube was another big influence. It's like a news show but for science, so they had episodes about places like West Virginia where the coal companies do mountaintop removal and thousands of people get cancer every year as a result of being exposed to these insane carcinogens like arsenic and other heavy metals, but nothing is being done about it because of the coal lobbyists paying off the politicians.

Vox taught me a lot, too. Their website sucked me in because it's just so visually stimulating, but I stayed for the reporting. One of the subjects they covered that year was the military-industrial complex and why we have something like eight hundred military bases around the world.

What else? *Vice News Tonight,* that was a big influence, too. I would get up in the morning and watch *Vice News,* go to school, come home, grab some food, and spend an hour or two watching Hank Green or John Oliver or *Vice.* Then I'd do research on the things they said. It wasn't like all that stuff was new to me; we had covered a lot of the same topics in the debate club—I've had to argue about the morals of using airstrikes in places like Syria, about drone strikes, and affirmative action and GMOs and universal basic income, just a lot of stuff, a different topic every month, so we'd do a month of research on each one and end up being pretty close to experts. I learned to check my confirmation bias and prove my case.

Lauren started debate this year, too, so she can give you another perspective:

I was so intimidated by all these kids who spoke like adults. I mean, I kind of speak like that, but some of these kids sounded like college professors. But then as soon as they were done with the debate, they would go back to talking like normal kids. So I realized that you could present yourself in a way that makes you look more adult-like and still be you. Like, I do congressional debate, where they give you ten different topics and you have to choose affirmative or negative and convince the judge and your constituents to vote with you, which means you have to do extensive research on every single one to prepare your arguments. I've probably debated at least thirty-five bills this year so far, and two of the main ones were gun control and mental health care. We were doing those just before February 14. That's why we know so much about guns and gun laws and mental health and how the government works. So in a way, we've been trained for this moment.

Lauren took TV Production, too, where we learned about the news cycle and news pegs and second-day ledes, basically everything we needed to understand to keep our movement from fading out. So that's my message to all the people who said we're too young and ignorant to criticize gun laws—maybe you should try debating some of the ignorant teenagers at Stoneman Douglas. Just be ready to have your ass kicked back to 1776.

LAUREN WANTS TO MENTION the effect this stuff had on my personality: "One of the things that really made a difference was that David was forced to become friends with his debate partners and his TV crew. That was really when he started becoming a better person."

"Started" is the operative word, because it took a while. But those friends did help a lot. If you labeled them in terms of the school's caste system, they were the emo kids and nerdy STEM kids and later AP kids, people like Diego Pfeiffer and Ryan Deitsch and Delaney Tarr. We'd sit in the middle of the school courtyard with sweat dripping off us because there was no shade out there but we could have it to ourselves, talking about nerdy things like space, engineering, politics, and more space. Did you know that a black hole can not only bend light, it can bend time? *It can bend time*. So those guys really inspired me.

Eventually all that stuff combined into this huge ball of "David, you better get your shit together if you want to get into a decent college."

The teachers were really helpful, too, which I hadn't experienced a whole lot before. Like, I got a D in Biology in California, but my Bio teacher at Stoneman Douglas gave me a lot of help and encouragement, and I ended up getting an A. (Thanks, Ms. Boyd!) World Geography was another great class because it's a lot like taking pictures with my drone, an overview on the world that lets you see the bigger picture. I loved Astronomy, which is taught by a great guy named Kyle Jeter. He got me into researching the most economical way to feed an entire population on Mars, so I've been studying things like aeroponics and hydroponics and aquaponics. In three years, I went from all regular classes to taking all honors and AP classes and got my GPA up to a 4.2.

But it turned out that all the progress I was making in my education backfired on a personal level because it just made me a more arrogant dick, to be frank. I've been told this by multiple people. Debate people tend to be cocky anyway, so when I went into sophomore year and they made me captain of the debate team, I got even worse. Like once, a senior was giving me a hard time and I snapped back, "Hey, at least I don't work at Publix." That's something that I won't ever be able to take back. I sneered at him for working at a supermarket.

That kind of behavior pushed people away, and rightly so, but that just made me do it more. I'd make friends with girls like I had nothing but friendship in mind, then ask them out and get rejected and turn the rejection around—they were too dumb and shallow to appreciate me.

The worst was when a girl basically offered to pay me to go to homecoming with her—not pay me, but pay for both tickets to the prom, which were ridiculously expensive. I just said a flat no. And she was a new student at the school, lonely and isolated just like I had been and basically still was. And a sickening part of me took pleasure in it.

On top of that, I was starting to move out of regular classes into AP classes, so I had to work twice as hard to keep up. The whole thing ground to a halt in the spring semester of my sophomore year. I can't blame that on the pressure or guilt because I've always been that way—I start off at full speed and by spring I just give up and slide back down to the bottom. Then I start the cycle again in the fall. I guess I need to put myself in a hole so I can dig out of it, which is a stupid and inefficient way to build up strength. It's like stabbing yourself again and again to create a shield of scars.

When my junior year started, I was taking AP Bio and AP U.S. History, two of the hardest classes I've ever taken, along with Algebra 2 and English and all the others. It was insane. And I knew exactly where it was going—I would start with the same old uphill push and end up at the same old downhill crash. But I think all the chess pieces of my life had inched forward just enough to save me that year. I had a few more friends by then, better grades, and less self-disgust. And that girl who asked me to the prom would pass me in the hall without saying a word—she's never spoken to me again. Her face was like a billboard that read DAVID SUCKS in giant letters.

Then, finally, I got what I deserved. I met this girl who was such an optimistic, nice, kindhearted person. For the first time, I felt like somebody accepted me for who I was. This surge of optimism took over. I didn't have to be *that guy* anymore. I didn't have to prove how great I was all the time. I could be just another flawed human being, and she would still like me. So of course I tried to take that to the next level. I was all-in. For the first time, my shield was down.

She rejected me.

I was heartbroken. How could she not like me the same way I liked her? I couldn't blame her in my old narcissistic way because she was just too nice. So I finally felt the pain I had been causing other people and realized what a shitty person I had been, which made me want to get down to the root cause. Why did I keep repeating the same patterns? And while we're on it, what's the meaning of life?

I had to make a stand, once and for all. No more turning rejections of me into rejections by me, no more cycling between the climb and the fall. That was all just one big distraction I had created for myself to avoid this very moment, the moment of truth. So this time I wasn't just going to dig my way out of the hole, I was going to pile a mountain on top of it.

I decided to make myself as efficient and productive as possible. I started doing research on how successful people structure their days and found a couple of TED Talks on productivity. What I learned is that it all comes down to the psychology of motivation. How do you get yourself started? How do you keep yourself going? And the answer I came away with is whatever you do, you have to do it every single day, religiously, because that's the only way to build and maintain momentum. And momentum is the key. You need to get the ball rolling and find your rhythm first, but once you have the ball rolling things get easier. It's like push-starting a car with a manual transmission. You have to push like hell to get it moving but then it takes on its own momentum. That's what keeps people and movements going.

So I came up with a new plan: I was going to approach school like a Silicon Valley startup. I began planning my entire day in thirty-minute segments, literally charting it out on an Excel spreadsheet:

3:30 a.m. — Wake up, eat breakfast.
4:00 a.m. — Study for AP Bio test.
4:30 a.m. — Take AP Bio practice test.

The day ended with "8:00 p.m. — Bedtime."

My personal habits, same thing. Breakfast was always a bowl of oatmeal with walnuts and blueberries, no sugar, black coffee. Instead of letting my dad or mom drive me, I rode my bike to and from school every day, three miles there and three miles back. I'd get home hot and sweaty but I'd just sit down and eat, give myself a thirty-minute break to watch another TED Talk or John Oliver, then do homework and go to sleep and wake up and start all over again.

My grades started really climbing then. In AP Bio, the best grade I'd gotten on a test had been a C. Now I was getting some Bs. For the first time, I felt really happy. I felt like I'd found my rhythm and I could just keep going again and again every day. I kept studying and taking practice tests right up to the day of the final exam—and got a perfect score on my AP U.S. History exam, and a near-perfect score in AP Bio.

As you have probably guessed by now, a certain amount of that was distracting myself from myself. I was just so afraid of finding out I wasn't as great as I wanted to be. That's why I would always talk down to myself, even something as simple as "You're so skinny, of course the girls don't like you." Then if someone said that about me, so what? I had already said it to myself a thousand times. But it turned out that working so hard and keeping that momentum and refusing to let myself slide back down the way I always had before was really satisfying in itself. It was more proof that I didn't have to be that guy.

Finally, I started looking at everything in a different way. I had learned a lot from TV and school about inequality in wealth and class and race, for example, but now that I wasn't so numb to myself, I could connect it to my own struggle with learning to read. And sometime that spring I read *The Glass Castle,* which was and still is a huge influence on me. I definitely identified with the author being in West Virginia when it was freezing and she always had to kind of huddle around the coal furnace—it wasn't nearly as bad for me, but it brought back that feeling of being cold, except now I could see how good I'd had it compared to what Jeanette Walls had to go through. So I felt like, "Well, if she went through all that and came out such an amazing success, then I can do it, too."

Stupid as it is, I think it all came down to see-ing other people as people. That was the solution to a lot of my problems. It pushed me face-to-face with all the suffering in the world, not in an intellectual way where I tried to analyze it from far above, but this time feeling it instead. So I decided that had to change, too. Instead of putting all my effort into being productive and efficient, I was going to put the same level of effort into being a better person.

I went back to TED Talks I had skipped over before. There was one on the merits of being vegetarian, so I became a vegetarian, which drove my mom crazy. I saw a TED Talk on meditation, so I put that in the three-thirty a.m. slot on my Excel spreadsheet and started meditating for twenty minutes a day. I tried to reduce my carbon footprint by driving as little as possible and taking cold showers. And after a while, I actually felt a physical change—my stress level went down, I felt healthier, and my mind was clearer. And all that actually made me more efficient and more human at the same time. Which is funny, really, because I started out trying to be this super-efficient machine of world domination and ended up discovering compassion, and it turned out to be the compassion that made me more efficient. If you want to put it in practical terms, it's as simple as this: You can get a hell of a lot more done by working with people than working against them.

And those people who think you're more productive when you don't have to deal with other humans and their flaws? They're just deluded. You have to see your own flaws or you won't understand the flaws in other people, which means you won't be able to fix yourself or help them with their problems. And that means we'll never be able to fix anything.

Now I was even more obsessed with fixing things. What's the solution to the world's troubles? Well, what about education for women? I've always had feminist ideals because my mom is such a strong woman, and I'd learned about that struggle in classes like AP History and AP Bio, but now I was studying history and watching TED Talks about it, and I realized that every time women started to get more rights, there was a massive increase in quality of life for everybody. Women were the drivers behind the end of slavery. The women who did the Montgomery bus boycott kicked off the civil rights movement. In places like Afghanistan, economic and social progress always start with educating women.

I was also following the 2016 election, my first real presidential election. I wasn't especially excited about Hillary, to be honest, but I sure would have rather had her as the first woman president than another generic white guy who sexually assaulted and harassed multiple women and bragged about it on camera, too. Then I started thinking more seriously about things like climate change and social justice.

By the end of 2016, I basically felt as if I'd been trapped in ice like Lex Luthor and finally the ice was breaking up. This is just a little example, but I always wanted to be an anchorman. I thought I was so smart and talked so well that I'd be the Mike Wallace of my generation. But when I tried it in my TV Production class, I was just awful. So I started to focus a lot more on reporting and learning the same lesson—I'm not the story, I'm here to tell other people's stories.

And speaking of other people's stories, I'm kind of filibustering here. Lauren, meanwhile, was already studying school shootings in middle school.

IT'S TRUE, I WAS. Now, of course, that seems totally crazy—having to learn in class how to survive the school day. But we studied school shootings just like any other subject. It was in a class called Peer Counseling and it was taught by one of the teachers who—this might sound funny to say, but I know it's true—one of the teachers who made me the person I am: Ms. Rioux.

Every day, Ms. Rioux would play "I Was Here" by Beyonce, and ask us to listen carefully to the lyrics, and try to make a better world for ourselves. She would teach us about teen issues and problems in the real world. She would do a unit on drug use and she would do a unit on suicide prevention, then a unit on mental illness. We learned about the stages of grief, and we learned about what it's like to lose somebody. Like David said, we had a week where we talked about school shootings. My teacher made us watch the episode of *Glee* where they thought the school was under attack, but it ended up being a false alarm. I remember one day, I saw this PSA from Sandy Hook Promise, about a normal school just like ours, where all the signs of a school shooting that was about to happen were missed. It was a sweet story, until it suddenly became terrifying. And I remember that morning I got to school and Ms. Rioux was the first person I went to see, because the story scared me so much. *Is that real? Should we be worried?* And in all of her classes that day, she canceled whatever she had planned to do, and instead showed the PSA and had class discussions.

I was in seventh grade.

That's the same grade I learned in Civics class about lobbying groups that have so much power and control over our government. And I remember discussing with my friends about just how messed up that was—it's our democracy, shouldn't the people have the power? My friends and I were disgusted.

Mr. Grisette taught that class. The way he taught us civics was just beautiful now that I think about it. Every single morning he would put a question on the board. And the day's discussion would be organized around that question. I have my notebook from Civics still, I loved that class so much. And Mr. Grisette loved me back. I remember once I answered a question and he was so pleased with my response that he led the class in applause. I thought, "Wow, I actually do know stuff about the government," and it made me feel so powerful because even though I couldn't vote, I knew in the future I would be prepared to vote, and that I'd make good civic decisions and be active in our community.

Mr. Grisette treated all his students like they were his children. If Ms. Rioux was school mom, he was school dad. He cared so much about students that his hard work and passion made us hardworking and passionate, too. He really saw his job as training future leaders. I have so many memories of that time, and of that class. Alyssa and Gina loved Mr. Grisette, too. He used to call Alyssa "Giggles" because of all the joy she had inside of her, and Gina would dance in front of the class just for fun.

We were all so excited to go to high school, where we'd join our big brothers and sisters. Here's my big brother now.

THE SUMMER AFTER JUNIOR YEAR, two things happened—I volunteered at a retirement home, which helped make me more of a human being.

And I went back to California. First thing I did when I got there was apologize to that girl who thought she was my girlfriend. Even if it was way too late, which it was, it felt really good. I was finally doing the right thing.

The next little breakthrough came on the beach. I'd gone there with one of my old middle-school friends, and we were just sitting there minding our own business when this lifeguard walked over and started hassling my friend for putting his surfboard on a trash can. My friend didn't say anything back to him, but the guy was objectively out of control—he leaned down inches from my friend's face and told him to never come to that beach ever again. And it was a public beach! All that for putting his surfboard on a trash can so it wouldn't get sandy?

I didn't say a word. Because the real story was about the lifeguard and my friend, not whatever clever put-down or righteous argument I could throw out. So I just put my phone on my lap and tilted it up a little bit and filmed the whole thing.

What happened next was a huge confirmation that I was finally on the right track. My friend and I went back to his house and cleaned up the video a bit, then I put "Copyright David Hogg" across the splash page and posted it on Reddit. The next morning, that story was on front pages all over the country—and a lot of other countries, too. Then I got a call from CBS2/KCAL9 in Los Angeles. "Would you mind being interviewed about your video?" I was like, "Hell yeah, I'll be interviewed." But the greatest thing about it is that the lifeguard got investigated by internal affairs. That showed me the power of the medium, and that one person could really have an impact on the world. With a camera or a story, I could change things.

But my biggest changes were still ahead. When I came back to Florida and started senior year, I met Emma González. On first sight, to be honest, her shaved head put me off. "This is a person who's trying to be edgy." But we had friends in common and hung out before school, so I kept seeing her and noticing how kind and respectful she is, and my impression changed to "Actually, this girl with the shaved head is pretty badass."

Our first conversation ever was about memes.

Because in TV Production, we spend at least half our time making silly videos that could be memes—not cat videos, but goofy dances and funny bits of pop culture that have the potential to go viral. We just do that naturally in our generation. And I remember that Emma made a joke about "seizing the memes of production."

So she was funny, too.

We started hanging out and talking about politics and how messed up the world is. We talked about women's rights and the environment. We found out we were both space nerds and talked about that forever (@elonmusk, *please* hang out with us!). I knew I was obsessed with space because it's the ultimate overview, the ultimate big picture where you can see humanity as a whole. I don't want to put words in her mouth, but I know I also had the idea of being able to escape a world of such hate and anger.

Emma did talk a lot about how sad it is that so many people can't accept other people's differences. She said everyone needs and deserves love, and the most amazing thing about her is that she really puts out that love. I don't say that lightly.

She is the most loving and honest person I've ever met.

She was basically the catalyst. I started meeting other people and taking the next step I had to take—not just realizing that there were other people in the world, but starting to learn how to love them. I found out that it's important to be open with your feelings because if you're too busy hiding the things about yourself that you aren't happy with, then other people can't connect with you. I also realized that I had always had love for other people inside me but I was just too afraid to show it, and it dawned on me that relationships are really complex and you can't just go from one to a hundred like I had tried to do before.

I think we were all going through the same thing together. All seniors are probably like that, I guess. We're starting to become adults instead of just walking hormones. As Lauren says, we're starting to understand how to use our keys.

If you want to talk about the strange timing you sometimes get in life, that year I took AP Government, and we started talking about guns and politics. We talked about the NRA and the spot they put politicians in, not just Democrats but Republicans, too. It comes down to "Do I choose children's lives or do I choose to get re-elected?" But it was never about hating people. You can say the gun supporters are all old white men who have nothing better to do with their time, but it's still great that they choose to become politically active. Most people don't care or don't have the time. And a lot of gun supporters are basically people who support the military and the police out of some kind of civic concern, so that's fine up to a point. But this idea that they're big supporters of the law except they also want guns in case they have to rebel against the government and kill the police and people in the military? That's really oxymoronic. If you want to overthrow the government, you're not really conservative anymore. And it's the same thing with Democrats. You would expect Democrats to want people to have more rights and freedom and less government control, but in this case it's the opposite. It's like both sides flip-flopped.

We talked about all that stuff in class, and about the idea of a "well regulated Militia" and how things were in 1791 when the Second Amendment was adopted—we didn't have a standing army or even a military budget, so citizen soldiers were our only defense against foreign invaders. So the conflict really started with the Articles of Confederation because they didn't give Congress the power to tax individuals, not even to pay the soldiers who fought the Revolutionary War. And gradually we fixed most of those problems, but the Second Amendment just kind of got forgotten until it blew up over the last fifty years or so. Now conservatives don't even remember that the whole purpose of those citizen soldiers the amendment was talking about was to *support* the government. Now it's not about owning a gun so you can be a responsible American citizen, it's about owning as many guns as you can so the government doesn't take them from you—it's thrill-mongering, really.

So once again, all the things that were going on in my life kind of smashed together into one big thing. I felt like there were two ways you could live, by closing yourself off and hating people or by opening yourself up and trying to love them. And that led to a thing that still kind of blows my mind—the day before the shooting, I had this overwhelming urge to call Emma and tell her how much I cared about her. So I called and said something like, "You're such an amazing person, I don't know what you did to become so positive, but I know that you're going to change the world and I can't wait to see how you do it."

I'm so glad I made that call. If I hadn't done it then, I might never have gotten another chance. And that just hit me so hard afterward. It's another reason I knew I had to do something. You can't wait for a better time. Once you find that door, you have to turn the key.

Like I said, I can't speak for everyone. But if you asked me to explain how to use the key in one sentence, this would be my answer: We have to learn to love ourselves for what we are instead of hating ourselves for what we're not.

And then we have to love other people the same way.

Because if you wait for another day, that day might never come.

4

AFTERMATH: LAUREN

AFTER DAVID LEFT ON HIS BIKE THAT NIGHT, the night of that Valentine's Day, I basically passed out. I couldn't physically stay awake. The same thing happened the next night and the next night and on like that for weeks. During the day I'd have to take naps, then I'd pass out at eight or nine every night and wake up in the middle of the night, so I'd start the next day exhausted again. It's still hard for me to get a normal night's sleep. So many of the kids at my school are like that. I never thought trauma could take that kind of toll, but it does.

When I woke up the next day, February 15, my first thought was that it all must have been a bad dream and now it was a normal day so I better get ready for school. Then it was like a truck hit me—it was real; it was just yesterday.

I remember getting out of bed and going to the window. I looked at the sunrise and all of a sudden it hit me, "Oh my God, my friends aren't seeing this." That hit me so hard—my friends who had been there just the day before were never going to see the sun rise again.

When I went to bed the night before, I thought my two good friends were dead. At some point that next day, I have no idea when, I found out that two more of my good friends were also dead.

Everything felt so surreal. I don't know how to describe it. It was like everything was foggy, like I was in a foggy dream. That whole time is such a blur now. I know that David says I didn't stop crying for three days, and that he'd call to check on me and I could barely talk, I'd mostly just cry into the phone. I really don't know.

I do have a memory of him saying the quote that first night, the one that made all the news shows—"Please.... We're children. You guys, like, are the adults. You need to take some action, and play a role. Work together, come over your politics, and get something done."

And I kind of remember him on TV the next day saying that his sister survived but her friends didn't, and it was just unacceptable that these school shootings were happening over and over again. I was proud of him, and it felt good knowing that he was doing it to protect me, but at the same time I felt bad because I wanted to get out and do something, too. I just mentally could not do it. I was just kind of blinded by grief. So all I did was send out a couple of tweets.

I do remember going to the Pine Trails Park Recreation Center that day, the day after. It was a Thursday. My mom wanted to take me there because they had grief counselors to talk to us, but I just didn't want to go. I didn't want to go out at all. She pretty much physically forced me.

As we walked in, I remember looking at my fellow classmates but not recognizing them. We all didn't look like ourselves. None of us knew what to say, and none of us knew what to do. As we walked into the building, I remember looking at what my classmates were wearing, of all things.

I suppose it was just my brain trying to focus on something that it could control and understand instead of having to comprehend something so incomprehensible.

As I sat down with the two grief counselors, I remember thinking, "Are there even words for how to say this?" I nonetheless began to tell my story, which was hard enough, but harder still was sitting in that chair and watching the therapists weeping.

AFTER THE THERAPY SESSIONS, all the kids were filling each other in on things they didn't know, like some of the parents had to wait ten hours before they found out their kids were dead. Some of my friends went to the Marriott because their parents were at work—that was where all the parents of those who had been killed had to wait, too. Another one of my friends, her mom was really close to the mom of one of the missing kids and waited there with her until two-thirty in the morning, when they finally let the parents know their kids were dead.

On Friday night, they organized a vigil at the

park. They had Christmas angels up on the stage, seventeen of them. They read the names of everybody who was dead, and all of us started crying and hugging each other. My friend Jaime's dad spoke. He called her "the life of the party, the energy in the room," and everybody started crying louder. Then he talked about sending her to school, where she was supposed to be safe, and now she was dead. It was just awful. A lot of priests gave prayers. The sheriff was there, too, and some politicians, and they all talked about gun control, which was kind of good except nobody really thought anything would happen. I mean, they didn't do anything after Sandy Hook. So we knew they probably meant well but it was kind of like a bad reminder.

I ended up lying in bed again, trying to sleep and thinking about my friends who weren't at the park, kind of holding my own vigil.

Gina, Jaime, Alaina, and Alyssa, those were their names. Every time I think of them, I see their faces and hear their voices and feel their presence, like just how it felt to be in a room with them talking or joking around. I remember

Alaina laughing or Alyssa playing soccer. I wish all the people who say we shouldn't do anything could see them the same way.

So Gina, she was kind of a lovable nerd. She loved science, she was really good at art, she loved books—she was literally always reading. She had a really quirky personality, but the great thing about her was that she never really cared what anyone else thought, which gave her this magnetism. People just loved her. She would walk into a room, and everybody would go, "It's Gina!" We were in the same science class, so we worked together every single day on every single project, and it was absolutely bizarre how good she was. And we had so many conversations about what we wanted to do when we grew up, where we wanted to go to college—all my friends had those conversations, and knowing that they're never going to be able to do what we talked about, that makes me feel so sad.

Jaime had probably the biggest heart that I've ever seen. She loved everybody and everybody loved her, because she was the nicest person you ever met. And she was one of those people that can tell you're upset, even if you yourself don't really acknowledge that you're upset. Like, I would be having a really bad day and she would just look at me and ask, "Are you okay? What's wrong?" She was just so sweet and compassionate and cared so much about people. And God, she was so determined to achieve her goals when she grew up. She already had, like, her whole life planned out. She knew what college she wanted to go to, and she knew she was going to be a doctor. She even knew the exact place where she wanted to work. And she loved dancing. She went to so many competitions, we would joke about how stressed she was because she had to miss so much school. She was just an amazing person, the most lovable person ever.

Alaina was one of my best friends in school. I've known her for years because my friend Sammy goes to the same church—they're both Mormons—and Alaina was really into church. She didn't think she was smart, but she was so smart that everybody would go up to her with questions because she knew everything. And she was so funny. She could make the whole class laugh with one word, and if you were looking sad or tired, she would make a really clever joke about it so you couldn't help but laugh. I've been looking through my old photos, and I found a photo from seventh grade of me and her sitting at a table, making Valentine's Day letters for our friends.

Alyssa was the first person that was super nice to me when I first moved to Florida halfway through sixth grade, and she was one of my best friends all through middle school. She had this really infectious laugh, it was almost like her signature. In seventh grade, Mr. Grisette always called her Giggles. He never called her Alyssa. He'd be, "Did you finish the test, Giggles?" Cause she never stopped laughing. If the room was quiet, she'd just start cracking up, and then everybody would start laughing with her without even knowing why. I can't think of anything better to describe her personality than that—she was a girl who just could not stop laughing. And she was really, really smart, too. She took debate with me so we'd go to debate tournaments together. Sometimes I'd be so impressed with her arguments that I actually felt sorry for the people who had to argue the other side. And she was amazing at soccer, too. But the biggest thing is that everybody loved her. I can't say that enough.

Gina, Jaime, Alaina, Alyssa.

I'm just one person who was lucky enough to count these four as my friends, but each of our classmates who was killed had their own circles of good friends, their own special qualities that their friends appreciated, their own families who loved them beyond measure, and all these waves of grief just washed over our community.

I want to say one more thing about that, though. If you ever meet me, please don't tell me you're sorry. That's another upsetting thing I had to learn from all that's happened—you can't really console somebody who's gone through something like this. If you say, "I'm so sorry," it just sounds so pointless, or almost like you're trying to say, "See, I'm sorry, I've done my part." Even if you mean it in the most compassionate, best way, there's just nothing you can say that would make them feel better. The best thing is to probably just say, "I'm here for you." But then you should actually follow through. Because we're not stupid. We figured out pretty fast that some people are really just saying, "Okay, I felt sad, I'm a good person, now back to what I was doing."

I was thinking about that when I sent out my first tweets. Before that, I'd never used Twitter at all, maybe one or two times just to see how it worked. I wasn't part of the group at that point, just watching the news, but I knew people were doing things on Twitter, and I wanted to do at least something. So I sent out these:

> NO ONE SHOULD HAVE TO BE TALKING TO FRIENDS ONE DAY AND SEE THEIR FACES ON THE TV THE NEXT. THIS IS UNACCEPTABLE. THINGS MUST CHANGE IM FOURTEEN NO ONE SHOULD EVER HAVE TO GO THROUGH THIS. PLEASE JUST DO SOMETHING! WE DO NOT NEED COMFORT, WE NEED CHANGE.

> WE DO NOT NEED COMFORT, WE NEED CHANGE. THE EVENTS THAT OCCURRED ON WEDNESDAY ARE A DIRECT RESULT OF POLITICIANS INACTION AND UNWILLINGNESS TO DO ANYTHING AT

THE RISK OF THEIR POLITICAL AND SOCIAL STA-
TUS. WE CANNOT BE JUST ANOTHER NUMBER

The first funeral—Alyssa's—was the next day, Friday, two days after the attack, but my mom wouldn't let me go because she thought it was too soon, and that I might not have been able to handle it.

I did go to Jaime's funeral, though. Even though I was really good friends with her in school, I'd never met her parents. That was so sad, meeting her parents for the first time under those circumstances. That might have been a week after. There were a couple of others around then, too. I missed one funeral because I was in California, and I felt so bad that I dropped off flowers at her memorial and said everything I needed to say to the teddy bears.

All that time, I hardly saw David at all. I sort of knew he was out there doing a lot of interviews, so I figured he was just busy with that. I had no idea he and Cameron and Emma and the others were over at Cameron's house organizing as a group. I wish he would have told me, I would

have gone, but I think he was just trying to protect me and keep me away from everything. He
thought he should be the one to do it because he
didn't lose any close friends.

That weekend, our mom took us out to California because she thought I needed some time
away from Florida and Parkland and just to hang
out with my friends from when I was little. David
has a friend there, too, who's his oldest friend, so
he wanted to be with him, and he also was going
on the *Dr. Phil* show to keep getting the word
out. I went, too, and what hit me about it the
most is there was a Columbine survivor there
who told us after, "I hate to tell you this, but now
you guys are going to be part of this club with the
rest of us that have experienced stuff like this and
it sucks, but you're going to be in this club for the
rest of your lives." I just remember her telling me
that and thinking, "Oh my gosh, this is so true.
And everybody else that was there is going to be
part of this club, too."

On that same day, the day of *Dr. Phil,* we
found out that Donald Trump Jr. had liked some
tweets from people who were spinning conspir-

acy theories about my family. The first one was specifically about my brother and my dad:

> One America News @OANN Could it be that this student is running cover for his dad who Works as an FBI agent at the Miami field office Which botched tracking down the Man behind the Valentine day massacre? Just wondering. Just connecting some dots . . .

I was just kind of stunned. I knew about trolls, but that tweet was sent out by the host of an actual TV show, Graham Ledger. And it had a link to an article on a website called *Gateway Pundit,* and later I found out that President Trump had praised that website at some point, too.

The other one was from a guy who called himself "Thomas Paine," linking to a story on another one of those websites. The headline was OUTSPOKEN TRUMP-HATING SCHOOL SHOOTING SURVIVOR IS SON OF FBI AGENT; MSM HELPS PROP UP INCOMPETENT BUREAU, and the article referred to David as "the kid who has been running his mouth about how Donald Trump and the GOP are teaming to help murder high school kids by upholding the Second Amendment."

It's like, what can you even say? Because when you study this stuff in school or hear about it on TV, it's just some abstract thing that doesn't seem all that real. Then something like this happens and you're shocked. And you think, "Why am I shocked? I knew this stuff happens." But you are anyway, because it's just so hard to believe people would do things like that.

Then we left *Dr. Phil* and went home with friends to our old neighborhood, and I had to go to sleep again because I was falling asleep even in the car. The next morning, really early, something like four a.m., my phone started buzzing and buzzing. I finally got up and looked at Instagram to see why people were on there, and I saw all these white supremacists and neo-Nazis saying horrible stuff on my Instagram account, like *You're going to hell, you're an actress, your whole family is going to hell.* There was one that read, *Your whole school is not real, you're all actors.* I thought that was just so bizarre that someone would even think that. My whole school?

So I got really angry and I sent out this tweet:

Hey @FLOTUS you say that your mission as
First Lady is to stop cyber bullying, well then,
don't you think it would have been smart to have
a convo with your step-son @DonaldJTrumpJr
before he liked a post about a false conspiracy
theory which in turn put a target on my back

So that went viral, and I was surprised because
it really made me feel good. Just to know that
people were supporting us and they were really
passionate about it, that was kind of therapeutic
for me. Especially when people started attacking
me on that same thread. I was surprised by that,
too—mostly because the first ones were women
and one even said she had a daughter my age.

I looked them up to see what they said again,
so here they are:

@KelliPrewitt You mean how your bullying every
company who supports NRA? Pot calling kettle
black. smh

At some point, I got curious and looked that woman up. Her Twitter bio says, *love animals, art, traveling, DIY, crafts . . . spending time with family & friends*. Sounds nice.

Here's the one with the daughter:

> @spoutsmith And one day, when the govt has become tyrannous, you'll need a gun (or you can just throw rocks at the militias)! DUH . . . everything isn't about one moment in your life! You better get your shit straight little girl.

I told her I felt sorry for her.

Another thing I thought was ridiculous was how so many of those people who attacked us would say we were just kids so we shouldn't talk because we didn't understand the issues. Literally, on the day it all happened, that morning when everybody was giving each other flowers and hugging each other, I had Debate class second period, and we were learning about the NRA. Our teacher was telling us how they're the most powerful lobbying group in Washington so everybody's afraid to take them on, then we talked about how democracy works and gun control and all of that, and it was just a few hours before.

But the Melania Trump tweet is when I feel like I really joined the movement. I already knew about it from seeing things on the news and hearing David, but I didn't know what they were actually doing. All that time David was over at Cameron's, I mostly thought he was out doing more interviews. But one night, I'm not sure exactly when, I went to bed too early again because I was just bawling my eyes out and I got so exhausted, and I woke up all of a sudden and thought, "What am I doing? I can't go back in the past. I'm going to miss my friends, but crying isn't doing anything." So I went to my brother's room and told him, "I need to do something."

That was when he told me what was going on. It's actually kind of funny because the first time I met them all in one place happened because I was really tired again and wanted to go home to take a nap, but David said he had a meeting at the school so could we drop him off. Then he said he wanted to introduce me to his friends and took me in with him.

I already knew most of the people. Sometimes I would see Emma when I went to Astronomy Club with David after school, and I knew Ryan Deitsch a little because I'm really good friends with his sister, Sam. But just being in that room, the energy between them and the love, it was something I've never felt in my life. They were like a family. Not like when you say, "Oh, we're like a family, we hang out all the time." But really a family. There was just so much love in that room.

So of course, I had to join, too. And now, looking back, I realize it was the best thing I could have done. Just to go out and try to make change, it's so therapeutic.

We didn't go back to school for two weeks, as Stoneman Douglas was closed. But the middle school was in session, and so I went back to visit a few teachers. I really felt a need to go see Mr. Grisette. I walked up to his classroom, and knocked on the rectangular window in the door, and looked in. I'll never forget the way his eyes lit up. He literally jumped and ran across the class and by the time he reached me to give me the biggest hug, he was already crying. He was happy to see me alive.

The thing is, Mr. Grisette never really gives students a hug because he's always like "I don't want to be weird." He always gives hand hugs or high fives instead, but on that day, he gave me the biggest hug. And there was Alyssa's desk, and there was Gina's. Mr. Grisette has told his students that they couldn't sit there.

In a way, he didn't just lose two students, he lost two children. He lost two people that he loved.

THE LAST THING I REMEMBER about that early time is finally going back to school. And just like in Mr. Grisette's class, I saw the empty desk where my friend once sat. Not having her there to joke around and compliment me on my outfits like she used to do, not having her to smile at and share secrets with, well, that was so hard. And now, every single day I go back to that class, I have to sit there and try to learn next to her empty desk.

Nobody sits in those desks anymore. The teachers can't even stand to look at them. They're all covered with roses, like a memorial, so it's a constant reminder of what happened to the people who sat there. I'm going to say "surreal" again, because sometimes it feels like my whole class is gone. Like none of us is there, either, and the room is just empty.

5.

#NEVERAGAIN

WHEN THE POLICE FINALLY LET US GO, I hustled outside to find my dad. Kids were crying all around us, parents were crying, red lights from the ambulances and cop cars were flashing across everybody's faces, all this stuff you've seen in movies so many times where people just let it all go. But I felt this weird mixture of angry and numb. The one thing I knew was that I had to get to a computer.

I had footage—live footage from the classroom where I was hiding, even interviews with some of the kids who were hiding with me—and I was a "Teenlink" reporter for our local newspaper, the *Sun Sentinel*. I had to get it to my editor immediately.

To be honest, the whole thing still didn't seem real to me. When we heard the first gunshot, I was in my AP Environmental Science class learning about the different types of municipal wastes. Like Lauren said, our teachers had told us the school was planning an active-shooter drill with actors shooting blanks so we'd get to hear the sound of gunfire. I looked at my friend and I said, "Dude, that sounded like a gunshot." He said, "Yeah, it kind of did." Then the fire alarm went off, and we all got up and headed for our evacuation zone.

I was the last one out of the classroom. I think it might have been instinct telling me to be cautious because I sure didn't have any Spider-Sense telling me it might be real. It just seemed impossible. I remember saying to my teacher, "This is probably a drill, right?" She didn't answer me. That should have made me worry a little, but I just thought, "Damn, those are some realistic blanks."

When we got to the first floor, I saw a flood of kids running toward me and shouting, "Don't come this way! Don't come this way! He's coming this way!" I started running with them without even thinking about it. Sort of like, "Okay, this is what we're doing now." We found out later we were running straight toward the shooter. We would have kept going, too, but one of the guys on the janitorial staff stopped us and said, "Don't come this way! He's over here!"

At that exact moment, Ashley Kurth opened up the door to her classroom. Sixty or seventy of us jammed into her room in about thirty seconds. One girl was having a panic attack, but Chef Kurth kept saying, "It's just a drill, it's fine, it's just a drill," and I guess everybody wanted to believe her because we all calmed down pretty fast, weird as that sounds. Maybe we'd just had too many active-shooter drills—aside from the upgrade in realistic details, this one was just part of our routine.

I found a place to sit and tried to call Lauren. I couldn't get a signal, but it's always hard to get a signal at our school. I tried to get online to check the news and couldn't manage that, either, but our school blocks all the search engines except Bing, so that was no surprise. And we all knew from the other drills what we were supposed to do in that kind of scenario—lock the doors and wait for the police.

Then I heard the *thud-thud-thud* of the helicopters. They must send out some kind of ultrasonic vibration because I could feel them, too. It's so eerie, even when I hear them now. It's like the thud is coming from inside your body. And for that one split second, I felt the cold rush of fear race down my spine and thought, "Oh shit, what if this is actually real?"

So many things run through your head in a situation like that. Part of me was thinking, "I'm going to die," another part was thinking, "I'm not going to die; this is just a drill," another part was thinking, "If I die here, hopefully our voices carry on," and somewhere in there I remembered that thing my teacher had told me about the billions and billions of people who have lived on this planet since human life began—all those bit players—and we only remember a few hundred of them. All the other people are just background characters who melt back into the nothingness of time and the universe.

Honestly, I don't know what I would have done if I hadn't been meditating so much that year. I could have had a panic attack or tried to run out of the classroom. But I focused on my breath and relaxed my shoulders and listened for that inner voice. And without even thinking about it, I pulled out my phone and started filming.

That was probably the best thing I could have done. Ever since I bought that GoPro, having a camera in my hand has calmed me down. Anytime I felt awkward or out of place, I'd just start recording. Then I could think about lighting and angles and get into the flow. When I first moved to Florida and felt like such a misfit and outsider, the camera was like my passport. "I have a reason for being here," it said. "I know what I'm doing." And when I started taking reporting seriously, I found out that you can go up to pretty much anybody and say, "I work for the school news at Stoneman Douglas, can I ask you a few questions?" Everybody says yes, even police officers and politicians. It's like a secret power.

But now I had another problem. I couldn't just

stick my phone in people's faces and make them more traumatized than they already were. I'd never covered fires or car wrecks or anything like that, so I had no idea how professional reporters behave in those situations. This was the first time I ever had to contemplate how to cover suffering as a journalist. I felt almost paralyzed for a minute. What was I going to do, pan across the walls? And even if I did stick my phone in their faces, what would I ask them? "How do you feel?" What were they going to say? "I'm scared"? "I'm angry"? That's like putting "flammable" on a jar to show you how it feels to be on fire.

But paralysis was not an option. An extreme event can be a turning point that defines your whole life, or so I've learned from pretty much every movie I've ever seen. If I lost my momentum now, I might lose it forever.

The only thing I could think of was to turn the camera on myself and describe what was going on, but that was a scary thought. I already knew I was kind of bad at it, but I couldn't come up with anything else. I was just going to have to try to be as professional as I could possibly be.

I pushed the record button. "So right now we're in the school, an active shooter, it's not a drill," I said. Then I gave the exact time, described the gunshots and said we thought it was a drill at first. That felt pretty good. There's a reason why a reporter shouldn't be the story—it turns out, levelheaded observer is a much better look.

Then I ran out of things to say.

A few minutes later, someone got Internet access and pulled up some live reports, so I did a "breaking news" thing where I said the suspect had been identified as a senior named Nikolas Cruz—and here I have to give my teachers credit for drumming journalism maxims like "stick to the known facts" and "don't get ahead of the story" into my head, because I remembered to say that it hadn't been confirmed (which is good, because of course Cruz wasn't a senior). Just saying that made me a little more confident. I was old-school, I was going by the book, maybe I even knew what I was doing. "Again, this has not been confirmed," I repeated.

By that time, we figured the cops must have wrapped everything up and we just had to wait for them to get around to us, so I finally tried to interview some of the other kids. Most of them already had well-developed opinions on gun control, which isn't too surprising since they all knew about Sandy Hook and Virginia Tech and Columbine. "If you looked around this closet and saw everybody just hiding together," one girl said, "you would know that this shouldn't be happening anymore and that it doesn't deserve to happen to anyone, and no amount of money should make it more easily accessible to get guns." But the best one was with a girl who'd been planning to celebrate her eighteenth birthday at a gun range. "I wanted to be a junior NRA member," she said. "I was always fascinated by guns as a young girl." She'd even been to gun-rights rallies.

But that was three hours ago. "This experience was so traumatizing," she said, "I can't fathom the idea of a gun in my house . . . to have a bullet pointed at me, my school, my classmates, my teachers, my mentors, it's just—it's definitely eye-opening."

But one thing that she said in that interview absolutely burned itself into my mind:

I even texted my sisters, *Shooting at my school, I am safe.* They both responded with *OMG, LOL, you're funny.*

When I heard that, my instant reaction was, "That's it! She nailed it!" That one little anecdote captures the insane reality my generation grew up in perfectly—school shootings and mass murders have become such a normal part of our reality that we crack jokes about them.

But I get it. Even after experiencing it myself, I'm not sure it will ever be real to me. It's just so bizarre and wrong that these things are acceptable on any level, you go into a kind of waking dream. In fact, sadly, that's probably why I've been able to cope. People keep telling me that I just haven't started grieving yet, but I don't want to grieve. I don't want to go through the five stages that end up at acceptance—not now, not ever.

When I got in the car that day, I screamed the whole way home.

I didn't think about it, it just came over me in a rush—"Jesus Christ, it really happened!" But it was more a feeling than a thought, if that makes sense. And when that feeling hit me, I just started screaming "fuck" over and over again, which kind of helped turn the shocked feeling into something I understood better. I was so angry, super angry, angrier than I'd ever been, pounding on the dashboard and screaming *"fuck fuck fuck fuck fuck!"*

At that point, they still hadn't confirmed any deaths. My dad had stayed at the school to wait for Lauren, and I went home to upload my footage.

Action is therapeutic.

I knew I was doing the best thing I could, so I just did my job and pushed the rest of it out of my mind. Not consciously, almost like an instinct. Same thing when I went back to the school after Lauren got home and started that hysterical crying—I thought I left because I felt this sense of mission to get the word out, plus I needed to get some shots of the ambulances and police to cut into my live footage so my report would be as effective as possible. At most, I might have thought I felt some kind of survivor's guilt, especially because I wasn't really friends with any of the people who died. It took a couple of weeks and multiple sessions with the therapist before I realized it was really about avoiding my sister. I just couldn't stand to be around her when she was crying like that in a scenario where I couldn't do anything to make it better.

Lauren cried for the next three days, pretty much nonstop. And it wasn't the usual kind of crying you hear—it was Greek tragedy, rending-of-garments type stuff. My mom wanted to take her to the emergency room but Lauren wouldn't go. She'd just howl and weep and fall asleep and wake up and start all over again. I would call, and my mom would answer, and I'd ask her to put Lauren on the phone, and I'd stand there listening to her try to talk in between the sobs.

I didn't feel awful. I didn't really feel anything. I just knew I had to be there. So I kept going out and doing interviews like I was on a mission to get through the day. I don't remember a lot of those interviews, which is probably a good thing. I know I repeated the "we're the kids, you're the adults" line a lot because it seemed to work the first time, and I know I made a little dig at President Trump because of all the blowback afterward—but the first thing he tweeted was *My prayers and condolences to the families of the victims of the terrible Florida shooting.* Really? That's it? The same thing you said after Las Vegas and Sutherland Springs? After taking $21 million from the NRA for your campaign? Do you know about this thing called Google?

I thought I was pretty restrained, actually. I didn't even mention his name, just said that prayers were great but taking action would be better.

The conspiracy theorists had already started in on us by that time—kids were literally still looking for their parents outside the school when the trolls on 4chan started saying Parkland was a "false flag" and we were all actors. There isn't a single person my age who doesn't know who Alex Jones is and what he did to the Sandy Hook families, so that was no surprise. The only reason I'm mentioning it now is because my little dig at Trump woke up the gun lobby's attack dogs, which weren't sleeping much to begin with. They come out every time something gruesome happens involving guns, to argue for more guns. The only difference is that this time we were ready for them.

Before I get into that, I want to say that 99.9 percent of the people we met in real life were so kind and decent to us. There were so many volunteers, police officers, ordinary citizens, and even a lot of politicians who were just as frustrated and sickened as we were. Thanks to all of you! You give us courage.

But when you disturb a hornets' nest, the hornets only know one way to respond. We knew the attacks would get worse. It happens the same way every time—a bunch of kids get killed, then their parents ask for some modest reforms to gun regulations, then the conspiracy theorists and the NRA and Fox start ranting about the Nazi communists who want to destroy America by taking away everybody's guns. The whole thing is like a machine for triggering PTSD. And I was already running on anger fumes and those dopamine hits of human decency, which just isn't a sustainable model for any kind of long-term campaign.

So what was different this time?

For me, it started with Emma. She was friends with this kid from the drama department named Cameron Kasky. I didn't know him that well because he was a junior and we only had one class together, but I knew he was a playwright and an actor. We joked around some after class, too, so I knew he had a sly, kind of edgy sense of humor. What I didn't know was that while I was talking away on TV, determined not to allow this to become a typical two-day story, Cameron and a small group of his drama-department friends were quietly planning to rewrite the entire national dialogue about school shootings.

Emma was the link that brought us together. Two days after the shootings, I went over to Cameron's house for the first official meeting of the group. Aside from Emma, the only people I knew when I walked in were Delaney Tarr and Ryan Deitsch, who were in my TV Production classes. The other kids were all from the drama department. My first impression was "Wow, these guys are extroverted."

We spent most of that meeting talking about

what we wanted to get done. Being in TV and drama, we're all pretty liberal, so we didn't really argue about the macro politics. We knew that we had to focus on a few reasonable, achievable goals and hammer them over and over again, so we settled on basic things like background checks and raising the age limit for rifles from eighteen to twenty-one—Cruz was nineteen and got his gun legally, so that was important to us. We needed a hashtag that boiled it down, and Cameron came up with #neveragain. Some of us knew the power that that phrase already carried, and of its association with the Nazi Holocaust of the Jews, and so we used those words only in the most respectful way. And in that moment, there really weren't any better words to describe our goal: We never wanted this to happen again.

The rest of the time we just spent joking around and getting to know each other. It's possible that we also did a little venting about the NRA and certain media corporations.

People always ask us how we came up with our "publicity campaigns." The answer is, we didn't. We're really disorganized. Plus we're teenagers, so none of us likes to be told what to do. But that turned out to be the best idea we didn't have, because it takes a lot of individual thought and individual initiative to be that disorganized. Nobody asked for permission or approval—if they thought of something that seemed like it could work, they just did it. Some people did a lot of interviews; some people were really good at Twitter; other people focused on organizing and coordinating.

We were insanely obsessive from day one. We didn't really think about why we were so driven, although it was blindingly obvious later. We just got up every day and kept going until we fell asleep. Some of us didn't even go home. We just stayed at Cameron's house, sleeping on the couch or the floor and jumping up in the middle of the night with another idea.

Here's a snapshot: Three or four days after the shooting, I was sleeping on Cameron's couch and I woke up at one a.m. for a live interview on the BBC and noticed a bedsheet on the floor. I went back to sleep and got up at seven a.m. to do another live hit on CNN from school, and I looked over and saw the bedsheet again and thought, "What is that thing under the bedsheet—oh wait, it's Emma." So I woke her up and we started to go to the interview together, but she couldn't find her shoes and I tried to help her and we still couldn't find them, so we ended up running out in what we were wearing, me in the clothes I slept in and Emma in her pajamas, basically. We got there just in time and suddenly we were on national TV—and Emma was still barefoot.

We knew the odds were against us—if people could shrug off Sandy Hook and twenty dead first-graders, what chance did we have? But something happened that Saturday that changed that equation, at least for me. A couple of us had just finished doing a morning talk show on one of the local TV stations when they offered to buy us some pizza and give us a ride. Cameron and some other kids were waiting at a park to talk about our next move, so we asked them to drop us there. So far, so good. But after the meeting started, one of the kids said he wanted to pray. We said sure, go ahead, and the kid starts praying for us to find the compassion to forgive Nikolas

Cruz. Our attitude was "Okay, fine, hope he finishes soon," but suddenly this older man starts flipping out and screaming, "This is ridiculous, this is stupid, you're just kids, you don't know what you're doing." I don't know if he was the father of one of the victims or a friend or just some guy who happened to be in the park, but all of a sudden everybody started getting angry and shouting at each other, and it escalated so fast that it looked like people were going to start punching each other out—I'm not kidding, it was getting scary. And of course there was media there, so you could see the headlines: PARKLAND TEENS CALL FOR PEACE, START RIOT. That could have ended us and all of our good intentions right there.

But this is what happened instead: Cameron and I climbed up on the tables and screamed, "EVERYBODY SHUT UP!" And when they settled down a little, we just started talking off the top of our heads. These aren't the exact words, but basically we told them that hatred and division were what got us here in the first place and we have to do better than that. We kept on babbling and pleading and pretty soon everyone calmed down.

I don't know about Cameron, but I was on the verge of tears. If something like this could happen just four days after a massacre, we were basically doomed. But looking back, I think that was our first test of fire and we passed. The message worked.

But what about the angry man? If we were going to talk about healing divisions, he'd be a good place to start.

On the other hand, who wants to talk to an angry man?

I had to force myself, but I went over to him and said something like, "Sir, I know you're angry and you're suffering—we all are—but your anger is just making the situation worse." Except it wasn't that coherent because I was still five seconds from falling apart and the odds of him punching me in the face seemed pretty good.

Instead he just got this really sad expression on his face and said, "I know."

That was such a great moment. I walked away thinking, "Maybe this will work. Maybe we can actually find a way to keep people from ripping each other's throats out." Then I went to my friend's car because I had to go to an interview with a Canadian TV station and just as I was getting in, a delivery man runs up and says, "Are you David Hogg? I have fifteen pizzas for you."

I said the first thing that came into my mind— "Give them to the people over there, but make sure they hug each other first."

SO THAT'S PART ONE of the story. Part two is my interview with the reporter from CBC, who asked me if I'd gotten any death threats. I was kind of thrown for a minute, so he said it again. "Have you gotten any death threats?"

I said I hadn't, which was true at that time. But I finished that interview thinking, "Wow, this is getting pretty big."

Suddenly, anything seemed possible.

We started by going to war with the NRA.

The NRA waited for four whole days before they started using us to go on a fundraising spree. Some of us started talking about how to react, but before we came up with anything, Delaney put out a tweet. *To every lawmaker out there: No longer can you take money from the @NRA. No longer can you fly under the radar doing whatever it is that you want to do.*

The next day, NRA head Wayne LaPierre hit back. *I call on every citizen who loves this country and treasures its freedom to stand and unflinchingly defend the Second Amendment, the one freedom that protects us all.*

Game on, Wayne. We started blasting out tweets the minute we saw it. Mine was a response to somebody who tweeted the name of a big mainstream mom-and-pop company that offered special discounts and benefits to NRA members. I can't even remember what it was now, but I saw that and fired one back. *Ok, what other big companies support the NRA? Let's get this done tonight!* A few minutes later, somebody else posted a list: *Hertz, Avis, Budget. . . .* Then all kinds of people we didn't even know jumped in with tweets and Facebook posts and phone calls and pretty soon, Hertz put out an announcement that it was going to terminate its discount program with the NRA. Then Delta Airlines. Then MetLife.

Of course, that started a full-on war with the NRA's dark legions. The conspiracy theorists on 4chan and Reddit had been calling us crisis actors since the day of the shooting. The death threats started rolling in. One guy said he couldn't wait for the day when he could hang people like me. They started comparing me to Hitler. Alex Jones did a whole show about Emma and me being Hitler Youth. I try not to give stuff like that space in my mind—"Don't feed the trolls" is my advice to anyone who gets involved in this kind of movement—but they got to me when they started going after Lauren.

Here's a taste just so you know what to expect:

Lorin S: "This is the most blatant false flag I've seen since Sandy Hook."

Michael Payton: "He's a fraud and he deserves to be thrown into jail for perpetrating this hoax on America."

MarkII691: "CRISIS ACTOR CRISIS ACTOR CRISIS ACTOR CRISIS ACTOR CRISIS ACTOR CRISIS

ACTOR CRISIS ACTOR CRISIS ACTOR CRISIS
ACTOR CRISIS ACTOR CRISIS ACTOR CRISIS
ACTOR CRISIS ACTOR CRISIS ACTOR CRISIS
ACTOR CRISIS ACTOR CRISIS ACTOR CRISIS
ACTOR CRISIS ACTOR CRISIS ACTOR CRISIS
ACTOR CRISIS ACTOR CRISIS ACTOR."

I had to trim that one down a bit because it literally goes on for pages.

My favorite post, just because it's such a ridiculous name, was from the "Social-Nationalist Meme Network." Which sounds better than the "National-Socialist Meme Network," I guess.

While that stuff was spreading to YouTube and Facebook, I made an offhand comment about my dad being an FBI agent. To the conspiracy theorists, that was conclusive proof that the Deep State had sent me to take all their guns. Around the same time, President Trump accused the FBI of being too busy with its investigation into Russia's connections to his campaign to stop Cruz from attacking our high school. A day or two later, the *Gateway Pundit* blog combined them into a glorious whole: My dad was in the FBI;

the FBI was Deep Stating Trump; ergo my dad was feeding me "anti-Trump lines." Now Fox had an excuse to do stories about the story, which meant the mainstream media had to do stories about the story about the story. And all of them wanted a comment from me—the sound bite everybody used was "I think it's disgusting, personally. . . . The FBI are some of the hardest working individuals I have ever seen in my life." For the conspiracy theorists, that was just more proof that Parkland was an inside job, so everybody had to write more stories.

There are two lessons to take away from that, future activists. First, don't let all that nonsense upset you. It's a distraction, which is exactly what they want. Second, they're just giving you a bigger stage—use it to upset them.

Also, make sure you have people like Sarah Chadwick on your side. When the crisis actor thing got going, she shot out this tweet:

To clarify, @davidhogg111 can't act to save his life. The fact that some people think he is being payed to is hilarious.

She's only sixteen, but go ahead and mock her spelling. Just be ready to duck.

Exhibit A: Senator Marco Rubio. About a week after the shootings, CNN hosted a "town hall" meeting where we were supposed to have a calm and reasonable dialogue with people like Dana Loesch, the NRA spokeswoman. To his credit, Rubio was there, too. After Fred Guttenberg, one of the fathers who lost a child at Parkland, tried and failed to get Rubio to answer a simple question about banning the kind of rifle Cruz used—Rubio said it was too complicated to separate hunting rifles from combat weapons, basically—Cameron brought up the millions of dollars the senator took from the NRA. "This is about people who are for making a difference to save us, and people who prefer money," he said. Then he asked Rubio to promise that he wouldn't take any more NRA money. And Rubio wouldn't say it.

Cameron wouldn't let up. "Right now, in the name of seventeen people, you cannot ask the NRA to keep their money out of your campaign?"

Rubio said, "I think in the name of seventeen

people I can pledge to you that I will support any law that will prevent a killer like this—"

Cameron cut him off. "No, but I'm talking about NRA money."

Rubio said there was "money on both sides of every issue" and rambled on about nothing for a few minutes, then Cameron asked him the same question again. And this time Rubio said he'd "accept the help" of anyone who agreed with his agenda. And Cameron said, "Your agenda is protecting us, right?"

What a disrespectful teenager!

This is why that matters—the dad had tried a respectful approach. He had tried to observe normal decorum. Even though he lost a kid, he listened politely while Rubio explained the infinite complexity of guns. We just weren't going to play that game, and history taught us that we had to do something different. I think Cameron said it best. This was a week later on the Bill Maher show. "We don't respect you just because you have 'senator' in front of your name."

Exhibit B: Sarah Chadwick, who fired off one of her killer tweets:

> We should change the names of AR-15s to 'Marco Rubio' because they are so easy to buy.

That went viral on Twitter and made every newspaper and TV channel. How could it not? And I guess being pwned by a sixteen-year-old after a seventeen-year-old eviscerated him on national TV was too much for Rubio, because he tried to fight back with a tweet of his own. Here's what the headlines were like the next day: MARCO RUBIO SLAMS TEENS AS 'INFECTED' BY 'ARROGANCE AND BOASTING' AS HIS APPROVAL RATING PLUMMETS.

Exhibit C: Laura Ingraham, who couldn't resist sending out a tweet of her own:

> HOW TEENS SPEAK TO AND ABT ADULTS: "We shd change the names of AR-15s to 'Marco Rubio' bc they are so easy to buy," Stoneman Douglas sophomore Sarah Chadwick tweeted.

Back to you, Sarah.

> I'm a junior.

A blog called *Red State* slammed Sarah for daring to suggest that the NRA bought Marco Rubio. "Over the course of his career, he's received a little over $3 million. That hardly qualifies him as 'bought.'"

Good point!

But let's put "Rubio Guns" into Google and see what we find. He voted against banning high-capacity magazines a year after Sandy Hook? He voted against a law to keep people on the Terrorist Watch List from buying guns? He's against expanding background checks? And this sounds familiar—right after the Parkland shootings, standing at the lectern on the Senate floor, he said it was pointless to ban assault weapons because mass murderers in America can always get one somewhere. And that's not all—let's see how he feels about laws to regulate online sales and close the gun show loophole. He thinks they'd put an "incredible burden" on Americans who just want to sell their guns without doing a background check?

But *Red State* was so smug and clueless, it just couldn't stop ragging on Sarah. "At 16, kids know it all, right?" Then they tried some teen-culture references. "This is her 'mean girl' moment. It's the equivalent of telling a rival on Instagram that her shoes are last season rejects."

Sarah's response? She divided the NRA's contributions to Rubio by the number of students in Florida, which is why thousands of teenagers at the March for Our Lives wore price tags representing the price Rubio put on our lives: $1.05.

Now *that's* seizing the memes of production.

So that's another lesson we learned. Respect wouldn't have goaded Rubio into baring his teeth on Twitter. And decorum wouldn't have gotten us on the Bill Maher show or CNN or MSNBC or all the other shows that wanted us to tell the story again and again. People really like the kid who finally says the emperor is naked.

While we're on that subject, President Trump must have decided his "prayers and condolences" might have been inadequate, so he went on TV and said he was all for universal background checks and raising the age limit for buying certain guns. He even teased Republican politicians for bowing to the NRA. "They have great power

over you people, they have less power over me."
Then he invited a bunch of kids from Parkland
and other places to the White House—one of his
staffers called me and I said I was busy—and put
out a really touching tweet about it.

> I will always remember the time I spent today with
> courageous students, teachers and families. So
> much love in the midst of so much pain. We must
> not let them down. We must keep our children safe!!

Then he had a meeting with Wayne LaPierre
and decided it would be better to have teachers
carry guns in school, and tweeted again:

> What many people don't understand, or don't
> want to understand, is that Wayne, Chris and
> the folks who work so hard at the @NRA are
> Great People and Great American Patriots. They
> love our Country and will do the right thing.
> MAKE AMERICA GREAT AGAIN!

Mature adults probably would have reacted
with some respect for the dignity of the presi-

dency. But we were just kids, what did we know? And more important, what juvenile and entertaining things would we say?

Twitter responded with new hashtags like #bowingtrump and #dishonestdonald. Kids jumped in from all over the country, and their tweets kept going viral and bringing in other people. They started making PSAs and posting them on Twitter feeds like #whatif, where kids asked questions like *What if we gave kids with problems counseling instead of detention?* A Parkland student named Sam Zeif did a great one about his experience in school that day, crying when he got to the part about his best friend getting shot in the head. People started following us in massive numbers—Emma didn't even have a Twitter account before Valentine's Day, but eleven days later she had more followers than the NRA. She has more than a million and a half now. And with each new attack, the audience for sanity grows.

Enter Trump Jr. clicking "like" on those conspiracy tweets and giving Lauren the truly genius idea of helping the First Lady with her campaign against cyberbullying. That went viral, too.

I don't want to make it sound like we were the central committee of the Twitter resistance. Other people were doing that long before we did. I didn't notice because I was a little preoccupied at the time, but the day after the shootings the Florida legislature decided to put a bill that made it easier to get a concealed carry permit "on hold." By easier, I mean they wanted to let certain people with special needs get a permit before they passed a background check. The guy who was pushing the bill explained it by saying, "This isn't the day to have that conversation."

People on Twitter called bullshit instantly. *Delayed till people aren't noticing,* one guy wrote. *Give them a week or so,* another guy said. We had nothing to do with that. We just gave them some hope and cheered them on, then they cheered back and other people joined in, and the whole thing started to gain momentum.

So that was another lesson—being yourself is actually a really good strategy.

Plus, it drove the opposition crazy. We just laughed at them and ourselves and kept hitting back, and we didn't put out canned statements like "I call on every citizen who loves this country and treasures its freedom." Instead, we just talked like normal people, or normal teenagers anyway, and thousands and thousands of other people wanted to join us.

The point is, none of that was planned. We didn't hire consultants and focus groups. It's just the way our generation has communicated our entire lives, and it turned out to be the perfect way to deal with them—you may have the Second Amendment and guns, Wayne LaPierre, but we have the First Amendment and Twitter.

The *National Review* said we should keep our mouths shut because we didn't know the difference between a shotgun and a rifle. The host of *Fox & Friends Weekend* said, "Spare me if I don't want to hear the sanctimoniousness of a seventeen-year-old." Another supposedly influential pundit mocked our PSAs. "The latest trendy thing to do is ask *#WhatIf.* It's mainly a vehicle for leftists to exploit kiddies into repeating their talking points. Unless you honestly believe a group of tweens launched a national campaign between shots of Tide Pods."

When that backfired, the bullies started whining. Tucker Carlson said the media was using us as "a kind of moral blackmail where you're not allowed to disagree or you're attacking a child." Good thing he stopped before he finished the sentence, because "attacking a child whose classmates were slaughtered at their desks" wouldn't have sounded as good.

Sometimes they just gave up and called us names—a candidate up in Maine called Emma a skinhead lesbian. I put out a Twitter call for someone to run against him and, to my amazement, the name-caller dropped out of the race altogether!

As weeks went by, we learned how to pick our battles. Fighting with trolls and bloggers is a waste of time. But someone like Laura Ingraham deserves it and makes a good symbol, too. She'd been going after us pretty much since literally day one, when she did a segment on how the AR-15 is the safest gun in the world.

But I really got under her skin with a PSA I made for #whatif. It opened with "What if our politicians weren't the bitch of the NRA?"

She responded with this tweet: *Perhaps if one stayed in school, one would know to use the plural.*

Next, she mocked me for getting rejected by four colleges. That led to a pretty famous dustup, because my response was to post the names of her advertisers. So many of them dropped her show, she gave me the smug apology that blew the whole thing up: *On reflection, in the spirit of Holy Week, I apologize for any upset or hurt my tweet caused . . .*

Man, did Twitter have fun with that. She ended up going on "vacation."

All that time, we'd been planning for the March for Our Lives. We were expecting hundreds of thousands of people to show up, so we needed money for planes and buses and hotels. When we started getting big contributions from people like Steven Spielberg and Mike Bloomberg and George Clooney, the opposition said we were the "useful idiots" of Hollywood elites and liberal billionaires. They didn't mention the GoFundMe page we had started, which brought in $4 million. Or the checks and letters we got every week from thousands of regular people all over the country. Here's one of my favorites:

Please find enclosed a check for the cause you personally have decided to take upon yourself. I cannot imagine how or what you feel. I can only say it should not have happened. We are supposed to elect responsible mature individuals for looking out for their fellow citizens. It's evident that this is not taking place. In fact if anything it's quite the opposite. Selfishness, greed, and power seem to drive individuals. For that we have mass shootings in our schools, theaters, concerts. I am sick and tired as I know you are from hearing 'our thoughts and prayers are with you and your family.' It rings empty and hollow. I'm sorry for your loss of class-mates and teachers. Please use this money for your travel expenses to Washington, D.C., or for anything you will need help with. Maybe you can make a difference and teach our so-called adults how to be adults. I admire your guts.

The letter was signed by a man from Alexandria, Virginia. Enclosed with it was a check for a thousand dollars.

Since our friends were killed, many things have happened that have changed our lives. We've spoken at Harvard, and gotten the support of some famous and powerful people, and we got to talk to Cher. But all of that doesn't count for much compared to the letter from that man, and all the people like him. They are the ones who have sustained us and who really made this happen. Really. In their own special way, the people who attacked us helped, too. And the 800,000 people who joined us for the March for Our Lives in Washington and eight hundred other marches in eight hundred places in all fifty states and six of the seven continents. When people make their voices heard in numbers like that, people in power listen. Here's a partial list:

- After Parkland, the NRA popularity numbers dropped to their lowest point in almost twenty years and big companies from Delta Airlines to Hertz stopped giving special discounts to NRA members.

- Dick's Sporting Goods announced it would stop carrying assault weapons.

- Massachusetts beat back a lawsuit to overturn their ban on high-capacity magazines and assault weapons—on the grounds that the Second Amendment doesn't mean it's okay for kids to die. Interesting fact: if you add up all the kids killed by guns in the twenty-three richest countries in the world, *eighty-seven percent of them are American.*

- New York passed a law to take away guns from abusive spouses.

- Vermont raised the age when you can buy a gun to twenty-one and also gave police officers the power to take guns from people who show signs of turning into the next Nikolas Cruz—that one passed unanimously.

- BlackRock started offering stock funds that don't have any connections to gun manufacturers or sellers.

- Background checks jumped higher than any time since 1998.

- The city of Deerfield, Illinois, banned assault weapons and put a beefy penalty behind it: a thousand bucks a day.

- In Parkland, Florida, Anthony Borges finally got out of the hospital. He's just a fifteen-year-old kid, but he took five bullets trying to protect his classmates.

- Within three weeks of the shootings, we were able
  to pass a gun law in Florida, one of the most
  Republican states in America with the help of a
  Republican legislature that's supported heavily by
  the NRA—sixty-three of them ignored the money
  the NRA gave them and voted for the bill.

- In Maryland, a Republican governor also signed a
  major gun reform bill.

- And for the first time in decades, two-thirds of the
  American people want to ban assault weapons
  again.

But just like we learned in class, when progress
starts, entropy rears its ugly head. Entropy asks:
How can we take as much money and resources
as possible and turn it into the least useful form
of anything? Answer: *Disagreement. Discord.*
That's what the universe wants, and that's what
we have to defeat as a society. It wants us to fall
into disorder and factions. Entropy is what the
guy who said that he can't wait until "we can start
hanging people like David Hogg again" wants.
Entropy is what the NRA wants.

Let's not give it to them.

6.

THE PARKLAND MANIFESTO

BEFORE FEBRUARY 14, WE THOUGHT WE HAD plenty of time. We wanted to do something that would make the world a better place, to fight for justice as lawyers or activists or crusading journalists, to be responsible citizens and raise goodhearted children. But first we had to finish high school.

After February 14, we knew how fast time could stop.

We learned so much at Marjory Stoneman Douglas. We studied Supreme Court decisions, read Shakespeare, and explored the mysteries of black holes. We spent a huge amount of time on contemporary issues like poverty and the environment. In our psychology classes, we talked about death and grief and mental illness. We debated gun control and the NRA. We spent a whole week studying school shootings. But it all seemed a little bit distant, a little bit like a dream. Either it happened before we were born, or it was happening somewhere else.

When it happened to us, we woke up. We knew we couldn't wait until we got out of college and settled into jobs. We had to make the world a better place *now*. It was literally a matter of life and death.

So we stood up and tried to make our voices heard. We're really proud of what we have accomplished so far, and are so grateful to all the people who have joined our cause. They gave us strength. They gave us hope. You give us hope.

But let's face it—it's not enough. And the merchants of chaos keep peddling their wares.

Sixteen days after we woke up, a man in Detroit who had just gotten out of a hospital where he was being treated for hallucinations shot and killed his daughter, her mother, his cousin, and two people who just happened to be there. Anyone who knows about history knows that the founders did not intend for anyone with an illness or a grievance to be able to take out their rage on the world with weapons that they could not have begun to imagine. This is madness.

It's almost summer now, and the death count continues to rise in America. Without a radical change in America's priorities and in our gun laws, our protests will have been in vain. Power and cynicism don't give way easily. But we have no intention of stopping.

After you spend a few hours hiding in a classroom while your friends and teachers are slaughtered, you can't stop thinking about how insane this is and how to change it. Volunteer in political campaigns? Try to fix the mental health system? Fight the gun lobbyists? Push for comprehensive background checks?

We think you should. We hope you do. There is a whole world to change.

You probably don't know who Tyra Hemans is. She was at Parkland that day and she had friends die. She was with us in Tallahassee when we asked our state legislators to do something.

She was with us at the march on Washington. She's a great speaker and a loving person. But we got famous and she didn't.

What about Zion Kelly? In September 2017, Zion's twin brother, Zaire, was murdered in Northeast Washington, D.C., by a kid with a gun. Zaire—a standout student and athlete at Thurgood Marshall Academy—was just sixteen years old. To honor his brother's memory and find meaning in his loss, Zion, who is as shy as Zaire was outgoing, has nonetheless made it his mission to stand up, speak out, and change the world. We were honored that he joined us on stage in Washington. But we got famous, and he didn't.

Or what about the protests at Liberty City in Miami? Four kids were shot there in April, and two of them died. One of them was about to get inducted into the National Honor Society. Hundreds of students turned out to protest. Only *one* newspaper went to cover the protest, only one reporter actually bothered to interview them. The TV coverage was shot from a helicopter, and made the Liberty City protest look like a riot. We got headlines, they didn't.

Those kids tried to make their voices heard just like we did. They lived through the exact same thing we lived through. But they don't live in a gated community. They are from a lower socioeconomic status and they are a different color. Instead of riding their bikes to school listening to NPR on their iPhones without even thinking someone might shoot them, they had to worry about it every day. In raw statistics, their odds of getting shot are twice as high as ours, and a lot of American kids just like them live in places where they have a higher death rate than soldiers in Afghanistan.

We're super glad people are listening to us, but we're not the story. We shouldn't be the "stars" of the school-shooting generation, which is a horrifying thought on so many levels. If people only listen when privileged white kids get killed—and even then, only when the number of dead kids is high enough to make the news—we're never going to fix this problem.

So what would fix it?

Once you start to think about that, you see how much bigger the problem is. At Stoneman Douglas last year, we spent a month debating the pros and cons of hiring more school resource officers. It would probably make the schools safer, but school officers call regular police officers to handle black students at a much higher rate than white students. Which means that students of color are much more likely to go into the "school-to-prison pipeline," too, which means they'll get something on their records, which means they'll have a harder time getting a job. And the chance that the prisons will do anything to rehabilitate them is slim to none or worse, especially if they go to one of the private prisons—which our governor enthusiastically supports, by the way. So it really should be called the "school-to-prison-to-life-of-crime pipeline." It's insane. We're actually making the problem worse. It's like we're living in a dystopia.

So what would fix *that*? Well, prison sentences are strongly associated with poverty, and a good education is the best way out of poverty. So maybe we should try harder to keep poor people in school. And give them better schools. Education for women is the best way to reduce the teen pregnancy rate, which is one of the best ways to reduce poverty, so we should make a special effort to overcome the economic and cultural obstacles they face, too. But where's the money going to come from? A rational government would take it out of our military budget, which sucks up more than half our tax dollars because it's bigger than the five other largest countries' defense budgets combined, but that means that you have to close military bases in states that fought hard to get them because they bring in money and reduce poverty. And do something about the arms manufacturers lobbies that push politicians to buy fantastically expensive weapons systems we don't need and don't use.

Sounds overwhelming, right? Probably impossible. When poverty and prison and getting shot in school are just some things you see on TV, and you don't think you could do anything about them even if you wanted to, you tend to tune them out. We know the feeling. It's called "learned helplessness." We were studying it in AP Psych a couple of days before the shooting. When you're in a horrible situation and you don't think you can do anything about it, you just give up. It's terrible that kids have to get slaughtered in schools, but what are you going to do about it?

We asked some local politicians about the school-to-prison pipeline problem back when we were debating an increase in school resource officers. They had no answer. They literally looked at each other like "Oh my god, I didn't even think about that." That's why we feel like saying "This is about kids' lives. This is about the future of America. This is blood being spilled. *You're letting kids die.*"

But the truth is, we didn't want to think about this stuff, either. We were forced to think about it because we couldn't accept the unacceptable. It would have destroyed us. And when you're forced to think about it and follow all the threads and see how it's all connected, you realize that people in power aren't any different. They're just bigger

NEVERAGAIN

#NEVER

RANDOM HOUSE
NEW YORK

A NEW GENERATION
DRAWS THE LINE

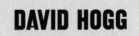

DAVID HOGG

(Class of 2018)

LAUREN HOGG

(Class of 2021)